Flávio Cardoso

Hope has two beautiful daughters: Indignation and Courage.
Indignation teaches us not to accept things as they are; Courage,
to change them.
(St. Augustine)

Author's Note:

This book was written in English, **in January 2015**, two years after the unprecedented street demonstrations in Brazil, without riots and vandalism.

THE MAGICAL POWER OF MOBILIZATION

Dedication

To my parents, who always encouraged me in business and in life, my brothers who were always friends and companions, and God who always illuminated my life.

SUMMARY

Writing a book is already a Mobilization

Every day I keep asking myself, even though I already know the answer beforehand: why are we so silly, so complacent in our corner that we don't react to so much that is wrong around us, to so many unfulfilled political promises, to so much corruption in public circles, to so many millions of dollars embezzled and to so many other acts of deceit and impunity that surround us?

We really are complacent!

If we wanted to, and when I say we I mean we - the people - we could put an end to a series of acts, infractions, thefts, embezzlements, corruption, injustices, exploitation and other things that are so wrong, that make this rich country of ours Brazil a violent nation, still full of miserable people, with one of the worst income distributions in the world.

Although we know about our potential, our wealth and the fact that we are already considered the sixth largest economy on the planet, we haven't managed to evolve far enough to be considered a First World nation.

All we had to do was want to and, of course, mobilize, and we, again - the people - could transform Brazil's reality.
We just have to stop, think, plan and mobilize.

I could very well be in my corner, living my retired life, traveling around Brazil and abroad with my income and the help of my children, instead of wanting to poke at people's sensibilities and provoke them to get out of their comfortable lives and take positive action to transform Brazil's social reality for the better.

I didn't accept accommodation and that's why I decided to write this book.

 Just getting out of your seat and taking action is Mobilization. Writing more than two hundred pages, then, that's Mobilization.

I may not change anything, only myself, but I'm going to try.

The problems are in us:

I believe that most of the problems of the modern world are in us, in our heads, in our way of being, thinking and reacting.

I agree with those who say that's why things often don't go well for us: we don't get promoted in the company, we're unemployed for a long time, we don't own our own home, we don't have a lasting love relationship, we have few friends, we lack money for almost everything, and we have the government we don't want.

What comforts us is that the problems we face and the solutions we seek don't just lie with us, or are our responsibility alone. There are culprits on the other side too, in the origin of the facts, in the incompetence of governments, in the politicians we elect, in the lack of jobs on offer, in the precariousness of the social policies that generate frustration. Insufficient housing, unstimulating education, poor public health and inefficient security.

The powerful don't want to change anything:

The capitalist world only wants one result from people: success. There is no place for underachievers. There is an economic model in place that cannot be changed, because it is in the interests of those who hold power, who have financial capital in their hands.

For those who are in power, who hold economic power, who have the rules of the game in their hands, new, revolutionary ideas are dreams, utopias, impossible to realize. If these ideas announce transformations, they are radical, dangerous, change the current rules, create instability.

The powerful do not accept Tax Reform, the Single Tax, the CPMF, Political Reform and Judicial Reform.

These are simple proposals, none of them the work of genius, and to be implemented they need political will, provoked by the awareness and mobilization of the people who believe in them.

THE MAGICAL POWER OF MOBILIZATION

Let's reflect:

Are we satisfied with the public services offered to us by the municipal, state and federal governments, which are civil and social rights, as determined by the Brazilian Constitution?

Do we receive good care in the health services? Both in the SUS and in the private sector? And in education, are our children being properly prepared? Are the lessons well planned, the schools fully equipped and the teachers properly paid?

So what do we do? In order not to spend hours waiting for appointments or in queues at public hospitals, which are free, or to enroll our children in city or state schools, where we also pay nothing, we prefer to sacrifice financially and pay expensive private health plans and absurd tuition fees at private schools.

Is public transportation of good quality? Why isn't there massive investment in rail transportation such as metro, monorail and suburban trains? Have we stopped to think whether the problems are a lack of projects, skilled people or simply lobbying, the strong political and economic influence in favor of wheeled transport?

What is our alternative? In order to get rid of the delays and discomfort of public transportation, which really is precarious, we opted to go further into debt and buy a car financed over dozens of months and be one more in the chaotic traffic of the big cities.

What about public security? Are we minimally safe? Does community and preventive policing work? Are there policemen everywhere, day and night, protecting us? And has crime decreased with disarmament campaigns? What about housing? How are we living, not those of us who have our own houses, but those who are less well-off, who receive a minimum wage, live on the streets, by the rivers and streams, at the foot of hills or hanging from high places?

Because we don't have and don't know how to demand mandatory public security, we don't react, we're scared to death when we leave the house and even inside it, we look for solutions on the simpler and more expensive side: we put up high walls in our houses, we buy cameras and electric fences, we pay for private security. And if there isn't enough housing, we pay rents even in slums.

And the people who run the country, how are they managing this nation? With ethics and fairness? Or are they deceiving us? What about the politicians we elected? Are we satisfied with what they do and what they earn each month? And what are they embezzling from the public coffers, as the press has denounced?

We complain, we criticize the perks and high salaries received by councillors, deputies and senators, and when the elections come, there we are, voting for the same candidates, or swapping some for others to do the same.

We are far from being an ethical and just nation, a lot of things are off track and need to improve! From the less than praiseworthy procedures of the political class, the complacency and slowness of our justice system, to our uncitizen attitudes, when we repeat shady acts that are neither legal nor ethical. In short, we collude with corruption by accepting the financial and character deviations of our rulers.

It is we, the people, the voters, the population of the cities, the municipalities, the neighborhoods, the favelas, who make up a country, a nation. It is for these people, for us, the Brazilian people, that politicians have to work. Really work! Not pretend. To think of a big country, which we already are, at least in size, rich, which we are without taking advantage, and strong and fair, which we are not yet and need to be in the task of ending misery and improving the distribution of wealth and opportunities.

Here in Brazil nothing works, no laws, no governments, no rules, no timetables. Everything is allowed, nothing is forbidden, anything goes to be happy. And happiness in this country isn't about having a lot, it's about having no commitments, arriving late, making an appointment and not going, working only as much as you need to and that's already a lot, not saving anything for tomorrow, what's the point, you'll die anyway, it's better to spend what you have and what you don't have, spending afternoons, evenings and weekends holding a glass of beer at a bar table, watching soccer, appreciating women. This is the profile of the Brazilian we are and what makes us different from other peoples.

Of course, there are exceptions...

Outside Europe, the United States and Asia, everything is very controlled, everyone is very well behaved and the laws are very strict. In Japan, politicians caught embezzling public funds commit suicide before being sentenced. Here, even with strong evidence, they deny it to the end. On public beaches in Europe and the United States, women wear shorts, you rarely see bikinis, beer is not drunk on the sand, on the streets, it's only sold and used in bars, if you drive off afterwards, you're arrested on the spot.

Minors don't roam the streets alone, as they do here, at any time of the day or night. They are picked up by the police. Prostitute girls provide their services unnoticed, they don't offer their almost naked bodies on the streets or beaches for any money. Here, prostitution is free and open.

That's why the gringos, the foreign tourists, love this country and say it's paradise.

Brazil is a paradise. We don't have a volcano, we don't have an earthquake and we have no idea how we're going to pay our TV bills at the end of the month.

(Author unknown)

PARADISE IS HERE

Is Paradise here?

It really is!

Whoever is correct in Brazil, walks correctly, pays everything, doesn't evade anything, plays the fool, the sucker, helps support politicians who do nothing for the people, just embezzle. This is the general thinking that prevails in many people's heads. Common sense, a primary judgment we know, but one that is quickly transformed into formed concepts, academic theses, prototypes of Brazilians.

Brazilians are cordial citizens, as historian Sérgio Buarque de Holanda once said. They are good, simple, cheerful people, who take everything in their stride, a people who are not at all serious, as Charles De Gaulle, the French president, once said about Brazil.

As early as the time of the discovery, Pero Vaz Caminha told the King that "this is a beautiful land, full of naked people and if you planted everything here, it would work". Pure truth. Five hundred years later, we are still a naked people, portrayed abroad as a paradise, full of soccer, samba and naked women in the streets.

There is a story told many years ago that when the world was created, God, together with an angel, separated the land on the planet and distributed the goods, riches and characteristics that each country would have. For Japan he allocated a small piece of land and lots of earthquakes, for the United States a huge territory, lots of snow, excessive heat, typhoons, hurricanes and tornadoes. For Europe, many small countries, little wealth in the soil, almost no forests, wars and deaths to deal with.

Seeing that only good things were happening in Brazil, such as beautiful beaches, a mild climate, no earthquakes, plenty of rich soil and the largest forest in the world, the angel asked permission and asked the Great Master:

- Forgive me, Lord, but I'd like to know why you're distributing good and bad things to all the countries and for Brazil the Master is giving all the best and no climatic misfortunes?

God put his hand on the angel's head and jokingly told him: - you're right. But just wait and see what kind of people I'm going to put there!

These "little people" are us, who accept everything, don't react to anything, if there's booze, women and soccer, everything's fine. The government can do whatever it wants, take everything from us, tax, confiscate, embezzle, steal and we don't care. We just complain.

The worst thing is that we like to be seen like that. And we contribute to it. No matter how wrong we are when we vote, we always repeat the mistake and every two or four years, we put people into politics who only want to steal. And we're left lamenting, without any reaction.

Unlike the culture of developed countries, here we don't have the habit of saving, what we earn is little, it's better to spend it all soon, you don't know what tomorrow will be like. This is how we think, the philosophy and rule of life of the current generation.

Young people, most of whom are alienated from politics, only think about consuming technology, they don't want to change anything, they prefer to keep to themselves. Children who don't take their studies seriously, don't respect the police, teachers or parents. For them, the folkloric Gérson's Law applies: whoever is cleverer, whoever steals more, whoever competes and wins dishonestly, wins.

Gone are the moral values of past generations, gone is the fear, awe, respect and education that everyone had for their neighbor, for the public good, for the priest, the Church, religion, the school, the teacher, the mother and father, the police and the justice system itself.

At school, a long time ago, when we received a punishment, a smack on the head from the teacher, we usually didn't comment on it at home, and when we did, we would get smacked again by our parents.
The teacher had all the authority.

It sounds like nostalgia, old people's nonsense, but not many years ago I still remember the respect we had when we entered a church and the ritual of making the sign of the cross as often as we passed in front of a Catholic temple. And what about the fear people had when passing a cemetery? At night, no way! Today, vandals, young people from all walks of life, attack and rob churches, raid wakes, ransack graves and rape the dead.

Churches don't stay open all day as they used to, they only open their doors during the few times when celebrations take place, and even Midnight Mass, traditionally held at midnight, has moved to 8pm. That's when it's still celebrated. In cemeteries, the deceased can no longer be veiled as before, late into the night, because of robberies. Generation Y, who live as if there were no next day, no future.

They want everything now!

We love celebrities. In few places in the world are television programs that expose and degrade human nature, such as reality shows, as successful as they are here in Brazil. From January to March each year, entire families, millions of people, are immobilized in front of the television watching sex scenes, degrading and contrived disputes.

All for money and a few moments of fame.

Soap operas of excellent quality, but full of nude scenes, explicit sex, homosexual approaches, betrayal plots and couple swapping are shown without any shame or restrictions during the day and in the prime time hours of television, from 6pm to 11pm, reaching adults, young people and children, who no longer sleep early like they used to. And for those who haven't seen it, there are afternoon reruns, with the same spicy scenes, without any cuts. Free for the kids to enjoy.

At the movies you pay and watch what you want. Free-to-air television is different from movies. It comes into our house without asking permission. And the whole family watches it. It educates and diseducates at the same time. And woe betide anyone who dares to go against this wave of media permissiveness, decides to rise up, promote a campaign, a virtual or face-to-face demonstration. Because of the dictatorship of the single discourse that prevails among those who dominate and have power, if anyone insists on being against it, they will be bombarded in the media, on social networks, offended, discredited, considered backward, homophobic, old-fashioned and an enemy of democracy. And if the citizen isn't a civil servant, his company will come under pressure, he'll even lose his job, he'll have no place in the market.

We have some journalists and bloggers who dared to speak out against it. They reacted, denounced, were condemned and are in limbo.

It's the law of the strongest: either the subject adheres to the all-powerful, permissive, one-speak current or they shut up. If you think differently, you become the enemy, the target of persecution and isolation, both personally and professionally.

In order to justify these libertine attitudes that we have here, they say that it's the same out there, even worse, that it's fashionable, that we're behind the times, that we're a macho people, that we're excessively conservative. It's a big lie, sold as truth to keep the emerging people, still uneducated, inert, subservient and doped up by the messages considered progressive. It works like this in the economy, in politics and in the lessons in social behavior that we receive every day from the media and social networks.

Anyone who travels to other countries can see that people don't act like this abroad. Although there are crimes and offenses just like ours, there is commitment and respect in attitudes, the laws work and there is exemplary punishment for those who break the social and constitutional rules.

Because of this and other things, we are at the bottom of the world, with poorer and smaller countries ahead of us, we are still a sleeping giant, a lot of wealth in the hands of a few, without knowing how to use it well.

For people abroad, and many foreigners who come here, Brazil is a lawless land, where everything is allowed, no one is arrested for anything, politicians are corrupt - and they are - women are prostitutes, you can pick up anyone on the street.

Repressed in their countries, where customs and laws work, Germans, French, English, Americans and Orientals fill airplanes, invade the beaches, especially those in the northeast, in search of free booze and sex tourism.

Here, foreign tourists, with dollars and euros to their name, find a full plate of facilities. Good, plentiful and varied food, very low prices, corruption everywhere, impunity, 10-year-old girls, made into young women, beautiful and available to offer a few moments of pleasure in exchange for money, gifts and crumbs.
It's so nice to spend the vacations here.

The only reason Brazil isn't moving forward is because the wheels have been stolen.
(Antonio Callado, writer from Rio de Janeiro)

THE BRAZILIAN REALITY

Brazil has always been one of the 10 largest economies on the planet. Even without realizing it. Today, it is already considered the 5th power, behind the USA, China, Japan and Germany. A technical tie with India. The latter, as here, contradictorily, with millions still living on the margins of society, as outcasts, below the poverty line, with precarious access to the minimum necessary to survive.

Complete misery.

The economic cake that began to grow with Juscelino, became a miracle during the military regime, and grew in size during the following governments, has not been shared equally by all. Instead of social justice, in Brazil the rich are getting richer and the poor are getting poorer.

They didn't follow Christian teachings.

There is a cauldron of problems boiling in our country, which inexplicably doesn't explode. A strike here, a strike there, a few demonstrations, riots, nothing more. This is due to a cordial people, an accommodating race, excessively peaceful, politically trained, religiously well catechized, so much so that even though they suffer the hardships of backwardness in body and soul, they accept and stubbornly believe that the facts are irremediable and that the solution to everything will come from heaven.

But it won't come!

At the moment there is a lot of violence, an uncontrollable increase in robberies, assaults, kidnappings, murders, financial embezzlement and political scandals. This leads us more and more to believe that everything is due to the impunity and lack of character of our rulers, and that the changes we want can only come through the people, through a real revolution, and never through beliefs, sects and religions. And it's unlikely to come from the political class.

Inexplicably, the Brazilian people seem to be sedated, groggy, sleepy, opening their mouths, with their arms folded, leaning out of the window of life, watching the band and history go by. And they do nothing, they don't participate, they don't contribute effectively to the social construction of the country.

They watch and face the country's serious problems, such as corruption, impunity, violence, misery, unemployment and unfulfilled promises without reacting, thinking everything is normal and accepting reality as if nothing could be done to change it.

This excessive passivity on the part of Brazilians is the result of the country's formative process. If we go back in history and do some research, we will certainly find examples to justify this disinterested behavior in the face of decisive events in the construction of Brazil. Traditionally, we have always allowed the direction of the country to be dictated and decided from the outside in or from the top down.

Few of the changes, advances and technological progress that have taken place in the country since its discovery have been achieved through popular mobilization. There have been a few localized revolts, involving corporate interests, with no major social or political consequences. The Paraguayan War, the Emboabas War, the Farrapos War and other historically insignificant events. Not even the Inconfidência Mineira had popular participation. It happened because of a few brave intellectualized citizens.

We left the colonial period for the Republic in a gentleman's agreement with the Kings of Portugal. Modern historians claim that the Cry of Ipiranga and Brazil's independence were decided in the basements of the Freemasons, where José Bonifácio was Grand Master and Dom Pedro was an apprentice. We ended slavery because of foreign demands. We went in and out of Getulio dictatorships in the 1930s and military dictatorships in 64, by coups in the dead of night, without a single shot being fired.

By political agreement with the military, we regained democracy in '85 at the Electoral College and elected a civilian President of the Republic in '89, after 25 long years. By presidential decision, our savings account was confiscated in March 1990, leaving us with nothing more than 50,000 new cruzados, which today would mean having only R$4,150.00 in our bank account.

It didn't work, inflation continued, people became poorer, life became more difficult, no one reacted as they should, only weeping, wailing, no stronger protests, business failures, especially small ones, a suicide here, another there, with talks, a good speech, new promises, everything settled down and stayed the way it was. And it still is today.

A lot has been given to us on a plate, out of convenience, subservience and corruption. We had our first university in 1922, the URJ, to welcome the King of Belgium and give him the title of Doctor Honoris Causa. The first Brazilian newspaper, "Correio Braziliense", was produced abroad, maintained by the Empire. The country's first printing presses only came into being when the King of Portugal was here and authorized them. The Gazeta do Rio de Janeiro, the first printed newspaper published in the country, was the mouthpiece of the Court. This was in 1808.

Later, during the Vargas dictatorship, other newspapers were born out of the wishes of the rulers, such as Última Hora. So too was the emergence of some of the television networks we have today, contemplated after 1964 by the military, in recognition and gratitude for their support of the dictatorship.

Brazilian democracy, now in force, was brought to us from abroad, copied first from France, then from the United States, applied in drops, now and then, a coup here, another there, always at the whim of imperialist, business, media, political and economic interests.

We could be one of the most important countries in the world, perhaps even the largest economically and in terms of quality of life, if it weren't for politicking, blatant theft, the constant embezzlement of government funds, impunity, and the mismanagement of the resources left over after the robberies.

Brazil lacks the political will to resolve things. Everything is too slow, confusing, postponed, left for later, after Carnival, who knows later, Holy Week is coming up, there are championship finals, the World Cup. Everything is left for later.

In reality, we are the country of make-believe. Everyone pretends to be doing something. And does nothing. They procrastinate. Politicians get elected, promise worlds of money and do nothing. Governments announce funds, guarantee work for the time being, nothing gets done, money disappears, no one is held accountable, no authority pays for the mismanagement of public goods.

Bandits assault, rob and kill, everything is recorded, there are witnesses, there is flagrant evidence and they blatantly deny it. The police arrest them, they take them to the police station, their lawyer asks for habeas corpus, the judge releases them, the criminal laughs and goes back to the streets.

Minors have all the privileges. They can rob, steal, rape and kill and they won't be arrested - you can't even say that word - they'll be apprehended, and at most they'll spend three years in a reformatory, a school of crime, where there's no recovery. Then he escapes, or comes out at the age of eighteen, without any convictions, with a clean record, ready to start again.

Start what again? A new marginal life?

It's a good thing that the people of the nation don't understand our banking and monetary system, because if they did, I believe a revolution would happen tomorrow.
(Henry Ford, American industrialist)

BUREAUCRACY AND TAXES

Bureaucracy holds back the country's development

We have the most bureaucratic public administration in the world. Unlike many countries, here the excess of rules, norms and laws go beyond common sense, dampen people's spirits and even hinder the country's economic development.

According to research by the Brazilian Institute of Tax Planning (IBPT), since the promulgation of the last Federal Constitution in 1988 until 2012, 3,510,000 (three million five hundred and ten thousand) rules governing the lives of Brazilians have been published. There are 35 tax procedures issued every day, including Saturdays, Sundays and public holidays, which makes the Brazilian tax system the most complex, unfair and bureaucratic in the world.

Our tax burden reaches 38%, making us one of the countries with the highest tax rates, behind only rich countries such as Sweden, Denmark, Switzerland, Finland and Norway, whose rates go up to 48%, but with an excellent return in terms of public services for citizens, who spend nothing on health, education, security and housing. All for free. Which is not the case in Brazil.

The Impostômetro, a digital panel installed in the São Paulo Commercial Association building, shows day by day, hour by hour how much tax is collected in the country. From January to September 2014, Brazilian workers have already handed over more than one trillion two hundred billion reais to the tax authorities.

The same IBPT surveys report that in Brazil, entrepreneurs spend approximately 108 days a year, or up to 5% (five percent) of their gross revenues, on supporting and complying with the tax procedures of the Federal Revenue Service, Social Security and municipal and state treasury departments. And because of this, we, the Brazilian taxpayers, work 149 days a year just to pay the taxes, fees and contributions demanded by the federal, state and municipal governments.

We don't actually work for ourselves until May of each year.

We contribute every year to workers' and employers' unions, councils and confederations, which give no return, we pay Income Tax, PIS, COFINS, ICMS, IPI, ISS, IPTU, IPVA, ITBI and many other acronyms and values that we don't even notice and which are charged indirectly on products or embedded in electricity, electricity, water and telephone bills, such as cleaning, street lighting, office and document issuing fees.

This paraphernalia of fees, taxes and levies that torment and enslave Brazilian citizens doesn't end there. In view of the deficiency of the public services provided, the Brazilian citizen still has to bear the costs of private education, health, welfare and security. That's another 41 days of work, calculated for those earning up to R$3,000.00 a month.

You can see and feel that a lot of laws are passed in Brazil, some of which stick, others which don't, most of which aren't well enforced, there's a lack of supervision, which is why impunity reigns. Many taxes, fees and contributions are paid here, just like in the richest countries on the planet, but the return is one of the worst, like in the poorest countries in Africa.

We are a giant country in territorial extension, huge in bureaucratic machinery, big in social inequalities, and tiny in our capacity for indignation and reaction.

Single Tax on Financial Transactions:

Brazil's tax burden is very high and there are many taxes, fees and contributions levied by municipalities, states and the federal government. What's worse, there's a complex bureaucracy involved in paying them and you have to keep documents for many years to prove that you don't owe anything to the public coffers, whether you're a taxpayer or a company.

Every day we see, read and hear complaints from all sides. Most of them come from businesspeople, managers of large, medium-sized, small and micro companies. The ordinary citizen, the buying customer, the service user, doesn't complain at all, he just silently laments and goes about working "magic" to survive in a country with so much wealth and yet so little growth.

"We need tax reform!" That's what businesspeople say, with the support of politicians and the agreement of the government. But nobody is doing anything concrete, anything that can really transform the Brazilian economic scenario. What we see is deception, the Supersimples program, threats to combine taxes under a single name, VAT, without reducing rates or simplifying collection. And political promises of a few exemptions for states and municipalities in a bid to win votes.

The Single Tax is no longer a dream, a utopia, an adventure, something that might not work. The CPMF proved otherwise. Copied from the Single Tax and levied for 14 years on bank debits, it proved to be efficient, simple, fair and non-negotiable, and didn't cause any disruption to the Brazilian economy. On the contrary, it raised a lot of money and didn't bother anyone. Its flaw was that it was used by the government as yet another tax.

The Single Tax model is the same as the CPMF. Except that it proposes doing away with most of the taxes, fees and contributions levied on Brazilian companies and citizens, applying just one tax with a rate of approximately 2.65% on debits and 2.65% on credits from bank transactions. In other words: a total of 5.30% tax. No more than that. And nobody loses, everybody wins. The government, which even increases its total revenue, and taxpayers, companies and individuals, who pay less and have their lives simplified.

A well-analyzed but stalled Single Tax bill, entitled PEC 474/01, has been in Congress since 2001. It would be enough for parliamentarians to ask for it to be shelved and to put it up for debate for corrections and improvements, and the consequent vote in plenary.

The Single Tax is so simple and efficient that it scares many people. With it, the tax machine is reduced, there are no more invoices, no more collection forms, no more Income Tax Returns. It's the end of bureaucracy. And tax justice happens.

Everyone starts paying taxes, whether they are rich, poor, employed or informal workers without a formal contract. Even those who do illicit business and put their money in banks start paying tax. So everyone pays less. And the tax burden falls.

It's true that no nation in the world has adopted the Brazilian Single Tax model. It was created in the 1990s by the brilliant mind of Professor Marcos Cintra, vice-president of the Getúlio Vargas Foundation (FGV). Some countries have experimented with similar forms of Single Tax, but it has never been applied to bank transactions and has replaced other taxes levied. In Brazil, we can implement it with total efficiency, as we have the privilege of having the most advanced banking system in the world.

Thanks to many years of high inflation.

The Single Tax model, certified by the CPMF, has been arousing curiosity and interest in other countries. It is already seen as the Tax of the Future. It has everything modernity demands. It is electronic, automatic, simple, low rate, efficient, non-negotiable, and its application is focused on virtual banking transactions, e-commerce, cards, ATMs and the internet. IU consolidates the end of legal tender, checks and paper money. And this is the model towards which the globalized economy is heading.

So why put off tax reform any longer, keep improvising changes, creating new taxes, experimenting with formulas that don't change anything? The authorities, politicians and legislators of this country need to put aside their partisan preferences and wake up to the world economic reality and have enough courage to innovate and revolutionize the Brazilian scenario by supporting the immediate implementation of the Single Tax.

In 1792, Tiradentes led the Movimento dos Inconfidentes (Inconfidentes Movement) to protest against taxes of 20% less than Portugal charged for gold found in Brazil. Today, we are taxed at almost 40% and we are unable to mobilize ourselves to complain in the public square against the authorities.

Everyone knows where the fortunes collected in Brazil go. Senators', deputies' and councillors' allowances, bid-rigging, embezzlement into phantom accounts. Health receives little, education almost nothing, home ownership only at election time. To hell with the taxpayer, Congress doesn't oversee anything, corruption reigns.

We complain in the press, tweet, send emails and texts to newspapers, give interviews on radio and television and even publish articles on blogs and social networks expressing our indignation, but we are incapable of taking to the streets and demanding change.

If we were educated from childhood to mobilize and take back our rights, an act of civil disobedience such as not paying all the taxes levied on us for a whole year would be enough and there would be no government that wouldn't surrender and make the changes demanded.

If we did this today, we could be beaten up in the streets and have lawsuits brought against us. But at least we wouldn't be sacrificed, hanged like Tiradentes was.

We need a People's Plebiscite. Before an uprising happens.

Education makes a people easy to lead, but difficult to direct; easy to govern, but impossible to enslave.
(Henry Peter, English thinker)

EDUCATION

How is education in Brazil?

It's going from bad to worse. Education is in its infancy, it's still crawling in terms of the content it offers and the quality of the teachers, who are poorly paid, unstimulated and terrorized by wild students. Towns and municipalities hold classes in the open, without even chairs for students to sit on. In many, there is no transportation and school meals are lacking, a major attraction for students to stay in class.

Learning comes last.

In elementary school, they've invented a certain Plural School, which doesn't "bomb" students, but promotes them to the next grades, according to their age. Modern Pedagogy, you can't fail students, you can't punish them, children can have psychological disorders and have consequences for the rest of their lives. There are many students in the eighth grade who can't read, interpret a text, do multiplication and division tables, and in college many who can't even conjugate verbs, interpret what they read, or produce an essay.

The initial proposal for the Plural School promised radical advances and transformations. Too bad it was poorly implemented and managed without continuity of objectives. Each city implemented the project in its own way, always for political gain. As always, education has never been a priority in Brazil.

There has been no progress in Brazilian education. On the contrary, it got worse. They adopted nine basic years of schooling and did away with pre-primary. Everything has remained the same. Nothing has changed in terms of content, classes are still unattractive, teachers and children are pretending. A setback for the country.

What will become of our future?

They wanted to involve the community too much, transfer educational obligations to parents, give pupils too many rights and take away the teacher's authority. Schools have become nurseries, popular restaurants, places for extracurricular activities and places for delinquents.

Teaching, which is good, is almost nothing.

Schools can't punish students or expel them. Children and young people bring guns into classrooms, threaten, shoot and even kill teachers and classmates. They go unpunished, protected by the Statute of the Child and Adolescent. An advanced law out of step with our times. Many rights given to young people, few obligations and duties demanded of them. Minors cannot be imprisoned, only apprehended, they need educational measures, even if they commit a violent crime, robbery, death, the sentence is a maximum of three years.

The results are the worst possible. Students who don't learn, teachers who don't teach, pretending to teach. Schools falling apart, without the slightest structure, governments paying poorly, teachers stressed, afraid to make demands, parents unstructured, with no time even for themselves, pushing children into schools. Drugs and trafficking are the paths offered to young people.

This is public education in Brazil.

If you pay, private schools are usually better!

The private network is no different:

Schools have become businesses. You pay, you pass. Colleges are springing up in droves, selling education and diplomas, buying students, without selection, exams or entrance exams. All you have to do is make an appointment. What counts is quick profit. The candidates' knowledge is weak, primary, obtained superficially in the first years of school. They don't have a strong foundation, most of them don't complete a university degree. They learn nothing. They graduate because the market demands it, there are plenty of places in colleges, quality, price and default regulate competition. Those who reach the end of the race get the diploma, but don't take the knowledge with them.

It's savage capitalism, which stimulates consumption, gives but cuts jobs, discriminates, demands diplomas and fluency in English even for bus drivers. What for? Teachers are required to have a master's degree and a doctorate, to dedicate their time to the job, their pay is discouraging, the market doesn't value age or experience, and the individual becomes a part, an instrument, a tool, discarded at the first sign of a financial crisis.

Mobilization in Education:

For education to improve, investment in the sector has to be a priority, quality schools need to be built, subjects reformulated and educators' careers valued.

Students need to spend more time at school, the ideal is full-time, they come in in the morning, leave in the afternoon, have breakfast, lunch and other activities.

Content is outdated, it needs to be reformulated, modernized, and subjects like history, geography and science reduced and simplified. Today, almost everything can be found on the internet, just go to Google. It's interesting to teach other subjects using new technologies, action games, which are a favorite among teenagers.

Education is a right for all Brazilians, guaranteed in the Federal Constitution. No child between the ages of six and 15 can be left out of school. It is the state's obligation to ensure this right.

What if this right isn't given, or is offered in precarious conditions? What should we do?

It's about reporting irregularities, taking the problem to the authorities, calling the local press, protesting, spreading the word on social media, demonstrating, blocking students' and teachers' access to the school, demanding immediate action. Protests and demonstrations are still the best weapons democracy has to offer citizens to demand their rights.

If we don't have quality education, if we don't form conscious citizens, how are we going to demand our rights, such as a health system that meets the basic needs of the population?

If education is doing badly, at least public health must be doing very well!

Excuse the pun: being killed by a mosquito is the end of the stick.
(Guilherme Cardoso, writer)

PUBLIC HEALTH

Public health in a coma:

It's hard to know who is sicker in this story: the people or the Unified Health System. Hospitals falling apart, abandoned in the middle of the woods, equipment bought and sitting idle, waiting for the public machine to unravel. Doctors earning little, underpaid professionals, people pretending to work, patients dying in the queue without medical attention.

There's a Russian roulette in healthcare, a choice of who lives and who dies, so great is the demand and so lacking are the resources in public hospitals. There are no beds for the sick, ICUs for the most seriously ill, and children and the elderly spend days and nights in corridors.

Waiting to hear who the winner will be.

Brazil has more than enough doctors. In the last census in 2010, the country had around 400,000 trained doctors. Proportionally to the population, we have two doctors per 1,000 inhabitants, a rate very close to developed countries such as England, which has 2.7 doctors per 1,000 inhabitants. The problem here is that most doctors are concentrated in the big cities and are not interested in practicing in the outskirts or in smaller towns.

In the countryside and on the outskirts, the health structure is even worse.

To ease the burden on the Unified Health System, the federal government is importing foreign doctors, paying them well and convincing them to work in the interior of the country, in poor areas with no hospitals or infrastructure. It's causing controversy in the Brazilian medical profession, with professionals claiming that it's unconstitutional, that graduates from another country need to have their diploma revalidated here and be fluent in Portuguese. There is a risk that healthcare will get worse than it already is. Only time will tell.

While the majority suffer in the SUS, those who can and have health insurance, make an effort, pay what private companies demand, and it's not a small amount, skip the queues at health centers, public hospitals, manage to be seen, at least they don't die of starvation.

Health has become a business, those who pay on the spot win, those who can't afford it die.

Dying in Brazil and outside the agreement, as Rolando Boldrin says, is the most common thing. People die all the time, every day, in every way. By malaria, dengue fever, hunger, in traffic, on the streets, muggings, stray bullets, kidnappings, trafficking, drugs, impunity, poor policing.

More people die here than in many declared wars.

Public health could be more efficient, more agile and more accessible to the population that lacks resources. It's not fair that people are dying in hospital queues due to a lack of adequate care and doctors. This is what we see all the time in press reports from big cities, while small communities don't even make the headlines. And there the health problems are even more serious.

Lack of care, appointments and beds in hospitals go against the civil rights enshrined in the Brazilian Constitution. There are resources. In order to alleviate the problem, it would be enough for a judge on duty to issue an injunction in each case of omission, forcing immediate medical care to those who request it, and forcing care to be provided in the private network.

But the law doesn't apply automatically. For it to apply, it needs to be demanded by those whose rights have been violated. For this, the majority of the population lacks a good level of education and knowledge.

And everything stays as it is.

As far as we know, the biggest problem with the SUS - the Unified Health System - is hospital admissions and emergency surgery. The network of public hospitals is insufficient to serve users with the efficiency and speed that many medical procedures require.

In private hospitals, the network is large and well-structured in terms of equipment, beds and specialized doctors, which makes care better for those who can afford to pay the high prices of health insurance fees.

Any proposals for health?

Here's a question that seeks a simple and humanitarian solution when it comes to health and saving lives. Since the public hospital network is insufficient to meet demand, wouldn't it be fair, politically and humanly correct for the government to buy beds and emergency surgical procedures in private hospitals to serve its users?

The taxes we pay are many and, if necessary, even the CPMF (Provisional Contribution on Financial Transactions) could return, as long as the proceeds went directly to health. As was once agreed.

What if the people who pay for a private health plan and are always complaining joined the thousands of users of the SUS, which is free but precarious, and organized themselves into a single front? They would have greater and uncontrollable power to demand immediate improvements in medical and hospital care from the authorities.

People are trapped in fear. We're afraid of everything, all the time.
As if we couldn't do anything. Fear is a paralyzing gas.
(Eduardo Galeano, Uruguayan writer)

PUBLIC SECURITY

Public security that's scary:

I miss the old days, from the 1950s to the 1980s, with little consumption, a lot of romanticism, precarious technology, a time when dogs were tied up with sausages, but there was security and tranquillity in Brazil. There were years of dictatorship, it's true, strong censorship and beatings, no freedom to speak, torture for those who reacted against the regime.

There was security for the people, thieves who were thieves stole chickens, they were called thieves, pickpockets, at most they took money out of people's pockets, they didn't kill just for the sake of killing. The people lived well. There was fear and respect. Of God and the law.

We used to walk the streets without fear, come home at night, no buses after eleven, fear only of hauntings. Today, people are terrified of the living, of their neighbors, of human beings who are more like animals, who have lost all reason, who attack children, girls and old people without mercy. Human Rights are on the side of the bandits, honest people are helpless.

No one can stand it any longer, people are scared, bandits run the drug trade, burn buses, close tickets, decree silence, impose terror. Police officers do what they can, others do nothing, there are the good ones and the corrupt ones in uniform, who, instead of protecting, prefer easy money and become criminals too.

Impunity takes over, criminals do what they want, they even manage the prisons. They rob, rape, kidnap and drag children down the street. Adult criminals, unpunished minors, use their age to steal and kill and not be convicted.

Militias are formed from the police. They protect bandits, partner with drug dealers, take money from shopkeepers, citizens are held hostage, become slaves, have nowhere to turn for help. If you shout catch the thief, you don't know whether to call the police or the bandits on the street.

The State has no presence in the community. Bandits are much more sympathetic, they play the role of government, solve problems, offer work, give pocket money, satisfy the hunger of those who are abandoned.

Traffickers provide for their mothers, wives, fathers and children in the favela. They deserve special attention from the bandits, presence, affection and money. He wants to go to the mall to have fun, shop, have a little party, he can't get in or buy, he doesn't understand why, television shows everything, everyone can, why can't he? Reality is different. Disillusioned, he turns to crime, he has nothing to lose, the moment is now, there is no future, his belief is in HAVING.

Lost and held hostage by crime, the government held a Plebiscite on Disarmament, lost badly in the vote, but still imposed the law, so that no one can have guns, legal or smuggled. The people knew what would happen, the bandits remain armed, crime doesn't decrease, in fact it increases and spreads.

Inland towns that used to be quiet, without violence, now have barred windows, electric fences, people attacked without compassion, robberies, kidnappings and ATM explosions.

No more tranquility.

Robberies happen all the time, on the streets, at home, in and out of cars, inside and outside banks. Bandits kill for nothing, blow up ATMs, rob lottery shops, take hostages, torture and have no mercy.

"Stay alert, don't react" - say the police. Robbers are cruel, they have guns, you don't, the law forbids it. The solution is to kneel down, pray, ask the thief for mercy, hand over everything, money, car and dignity. Waiting for the police is a waste of time, there's a lot of work, several calls, first the most serious cases, robberies with fatalities. Then vehicles and even helicopters show up.

Try calling 190.

The police also protect themselves, they're not foolish, they don't want to arrive quickly, they avoid confrontations, face to face with bandits. Police don't have weapons, bandits are better prepared. It's better to arrive later, turn on the siren, hope the criminals get away soon, nobody wants to die for free. The police are right, the profession is risky, salaries are low, the dangers are enormous, life is worth more. Bad luck for the people.

Certain things in Brazil are untouchable, they become taboo, many criticize them, nobody likes them or is afraid to talk about them, to debate what is right or wrong. Even if they are wronged or poorly served, people prefer to resign themselves, sometimes lament, and rarely mobilize to change what is being imposed as the best for everyone.

This is the case with public security and the ban on the use of weapons by good citizens.

The Magna Carta of the United States in its Second Amendment that, "the existence of a well-organized militia being necessary to the security of a free State, the right of the people to keep and bear arms shall not be impaired." In other words: there, the government recognizes that it is impossible to provide complete security for its citizens, and allows everyone to have weapons to defend themselves.

Here in Brazil, the opposite is true. Our Constitution says that it is the duty of the state to guarantee the personal and property security of its citizens. Governments fail to comply with the law, insecurity increases and violence grows. Good people are forbidden to carry weapons, while the bandits stock up on rifles, machine guns and now dynamite.

Every day, the press reports and surveillance cameras show the growing audacity and cruelty of bandits, both adults and minors, in the assaults, robberies, dragnets and murders they carry out in homes, stores and kidnappings. Without fear of anything, they blow up ATMs, loot shops in broad daylight and cowardly kill owners and customers without resistance.

For the simple pleasure of killing and the certainty of impunity.

There is no reaction from the victims. The police say they're afraid of confrontation, it's better to hand everything over to the bandits, stay on your knees, get hit in the face, be humiliated, see a child beaten or a woman raped. You mustn't react!

Bandits also know things, they listen to the radio, read newspapers, watch television, listen to the advice given to honest people, and they become stronger. Knowing that no one can have a gun to defend themselves, they easily enter any house, store or take your car on the street.

Often the bandits aren't even armed, they pretend, they put their hands in their pockets, they have a toy gun, they know you won't react. So he abuses, assaults, mocks, humiliates, steals everything he wants, turns his back on the victim and walks away, certain that he won't be arrested any time soon. And if you do get arrested, you'll soon be released, especially if you're underage, there's no flagrante delicto or you've been granted an injunction by some lawyer.

The police do what they can, but they can't protect everyone and everywhere. In reality, the police play the role of the SAMU or the Fire Brigade Rescue: they only come to collect the dead and injured.

After the fact.

That's when the questions arise from ordinary citizens, who don't understand laws, logistics or strategies, who live with insecurity at home and on the streets, and who are nevertheless better able to see other solutions to contain the worsening violence:

- Wouldn't it be better to share the duty of security with citizens, to allow, encourage and publicize the fact that now all good people will be able to have a legal gun in their home or business to defend themselves?

And those who disobey should be punished exemplarily.

Why not copy the procedures required for someone to get a driver's license? Want to own a gun at home? Take about 20 classes on safety and shooting practice, pass a mental health test, present a certificate of good record, and if approved, receive a license and authorization to purchase a 32 or 38 caliber revolver. And every two years be obliged to revalidate the license.

Since they can't take guns away from criminals, maybe by arming good citizens and training them to handle them properly, criminals will think twice before assaulting, robbing and killing? They will at least know that people are able to defend themselves, and that before they kill someone, they can also be killed.

Community Policing:

Violence is on the rise in the capital and neighboring cities. Accessing social networks, we learn of people's indignation. Assaults and killings, which are commonplace in the city center and in outlying neighborhoods, are now causing astonishment and fear among residents of the south zone, Belo Horizonte's noblest region.

Wouldn't it be time to improve the community policing that the Military Police never tire of claiming to carry out in Belo Horizonte?

Then they invented the Network of Protected Neighbors, a well-intentioned program, which on paper and in lectures works very well, but in practice is a great utopia.

Let's agree that in this day and age, rescuing the spirit of solidarity and good neighborliness in people is a difficult, almost impossible task. In reality, the program is nothing more than a subtle attempt by the Military Police to transfer to the communities the obligation to monitor and supervise criminal actions in their neighborhoods.

In today's fast-paced life, everyone has no time, no one knows anyone, you don't trust your relative or your next-door neighbor, seeking this solidarity becomes a utopia.

Today you have to doubt everything and everyone. You believe the neighbor, he says he's going away for a fortnight, the husband or son comments in the bar, someone listens, it could be the bandit, he takes advantage of the carelessness, chooses the day and time and steals everything in the house.

The community wants more men on the streets, if possible day and night, circulating around the neighborhood in cars and on motorcycles, which are much more agile.

Police on the streets, bandits feel afraid, people feel safe.

Why not be more daring, more creative, set up police stations in the neighborhoods and distribute the entire contingent proportionally throughout the city? Citizens want to see the police close to them, not after a crime has been committed. All you have to do is form partnerships with local businesses, gas stations, or rent houses in the neighborhoods and turn them into police stations, placing vehicles, motorcycles and soldiers there for constant, preventive patrols of the area.

What happened to the police kiosks set up around the city, many in partnership with the community? Most have been removed, and in others you never see a policeman inside.

And why not use more motorcycles to patrol big cities? With a policeman on each motorcycle, there would be more men distributed around neighborhoods and moving faster than cars, given the chaotic traffic in big cities.

I'm sure the results will be much better, the community will feel safer and violence will decrease. Not to mention the fact that it will be quicker to respond to incidents and will save on fuel costs, since the vehicles will circulate in a smaller radius.

In the model we see today, the police as a whole embracing the city, at most distributed in battalions, running back and forth after bandits, with traffic and huge distances, we know it's impossible to avoid robberies and deaths, which is why they almost always arrive after the fact, with several vehicles, even a helicopter.

I understand community policing as it exists in the United States. I lived there for three years. It's preventive policing, men and vehicles circulating throughout the city at all times. Day and night.

There, responsibility for the safety of citizens lies with the municipality. Each town has its own police force that reports to the elected mayor. And the community trusts them. In any neighborhood, residents can easily see police officers and their vehicles roaming the streets 24 hours a day. In addition to routine policing, they are also responsible for traffic patrols.

This is how the police should act in Brazil, and in this case, here in Belo Horizonte. Hire more police officers, give them good salaries, divide them into eight-hour shifts, build or rent houses in the neighborhoods to serve as strategic posts and distribute police officers and vehicles throughout the streets, day and night.

Police officers need to be based in neighborhoods, close to their residents. Assisted by technology. This is the only way to reduce violence and make citizens feel safe.

And why two police forces?

It's strange that there are two police forces doing, in theory, the same job of patrolling, arresting and investigating. One is uniformed, with clothes and equipment very similar to Army soldiers, who are trained and prepared for a possible war. Which hasn't happened in Brazil for centuries.

I haven't looked into it, but it's almost certain that only in Brazil are there two separate police forces, with separate commands and similar functions.

Disagreements between the two police forces are not uncommon. Almost always, one police force's outstanding performance hurts the vanity of the other. Especially when it comes to arresting the perpetrators of heinous crimes, which generate public commotion, or breaking up gangs of major drug traffickers. Each commander or deputy wants the credit and the limelight of the press for himself.

Why not just have one police force, with one command, one barracks, the same facilities and sharing the same work and security strategy? It's like that in the United States, I've read about it and we see it in the movies. There's the police chief, the civilian staff, with their positions and functions, who don't wear uniforms, who investigate and arrest, and the uniformed staff, who do preventive patrols on the streets and arrest people too. They all work in the same space, under the same command and share the same information.

In Brazil, each police force wants to do the best it can on its own, and neither can provide security for anyone.

Brazilian justice is very efficient at two moments: when it condemns the poor and when it acquits the rich.
(Author unknown)

JUSTICE

The tortuous paths of justice:

Can you understand the justice system and the laws in force in Brazil? There are many laws, most of which are not applied and therefore not respected. Justice, which is blind, deaf and dumb to the pleas of the poorest and most needy, only works well for the wealthy, politicians and the powerful. Just look at the list of politicians indicted for stealing public money and who don't go to jail.

I don't understand the intricacies of justice, I'm a layman. Like me, few understand or comprehend the paths of an investigation, the process, the appeals, the trial, and finally the conviction or acquittal of someone. Much less do we understand the motives and speed of so many injunctions and habeas corpus obtained by lawyers to free their clients.

Could it be poorly carried out investigations or loopholes in the law that make judges accept so many injunctions against successive cases? As an ordinary citizen, I think that the police and the Public Prosecutor's Office, before making accusations against anyone, should gather as much evidence as possible to be sure that a certain person or company is involved. Then they should file charges. And the courts, with hard evidence, should accept them, without too many challenges.

What is clear from the appeals is that most of the accusations against someone who has allegedly committed a crime, be it a politician, a military officer or a simple citizen, are being presented to the courts in haste and made public by the media, without any care being taken to investigate them.

There are cases, and there are many, in which the crime is very clear, there is a flagrant act, the subject has crashed the car, killed, was drunk, is taken to jail and is soon released by an injunction. Sometimes the accused is arrested, spontaneously admits to committing the crime, yet is released, to await investigations in freedom.

It's hard to understand all this legal maneuvering. Are the lawyers so clever or is justice literally blind?

It shouldn't be like this.

Wouldn't it be more correct for those who have killed, confessed to the crime or were caught in the act to be evaluated on the spot by a judge and then sent to jail, already serving part of the probable sentence that will be imposed on them at trial?

If the trial takes years, that's bad luck for the guilty, not for the victims or their families. It should be like this: while those proven guilty wait for justice to take its course, they serve part of their sentence until a jury decides on the number of years to be served as a definitive sentence.

It's no longer enough to see things the way they are, with the police arresting, the Public Prosecutor's Office denouncing and judges of all levels releasing bandits and criminals. Every day the people become more disillusioned and disbelieving in politicians, especially in the justice system, their last hope of seeing those who shamelessly steal, rob and kill, in politics, at home and on the streets, punished.

It's past time for a thorough judicial reform.

Judges apply justice?

We have plenty of judges, compare that with European countries. According to the National Council of Justice (CNJ), here and abroad the parity is the same: eight judges for every 100,000 inhabitants. In practice, it seems that we have so few magistrates, such is the disorder of justice, the backlog of cases, the delay in trials and the uncertainty of convictions.

Slow justice, a full plate for impunity.

Magistrates complain about everything and everyone, they have too many cases, they work too hard, poor things. They forget that they are paid very well, some of them exaggeratedly, more than a president, the salaries of maharajas, which the ousted Collor once tried in vain to reduce.

Judges apply the law, they seem to be the masters of the truth. They misinterpret the process, convict and leave openings. The police make an effort, arrest, the courts soon release, weak arguments, strong mistrust. Spurious interests.

Poor people know better, prejudice explains it, jail was made for them. Those who are powerful and rich in Brazil, have a name and a broad back, rarely go to jail, there's always a judge on duty with a habeas corpus available.

It's hard for ordinary people to understand why someone drinks a lot, drives at high speed, hits and kills people and doesn't get arrested. Sometimes they are arrested for a moment, but they don't stay in jail for more than a day. He is then released on the grounds that he is a primary defendant and should await criminal proceedings in freedom. Often, not even his driver's license is seized. And we know how long it takes for an offender to be tried and convicted.

And if you have money and prestige, this process drags on for years, until it falls into oblivion and lapses. This is constant practice and applies to any crime committed by those who can afford to hire good lawyers.

If the person accused of crimes is a politician who has special privileges and a special legal forum, it is almost impossible for them to be convicted and imprisoned, even if the evidence is overwhelming. If there is strong pressure from the media, the elected politician can at most be impeached by his or her peers, if he or she doesn't resign first, thus guaranteeing the right to run for office and return to public life.

We see this kind of impunity in politics every day in Brazil. Not a week goes by without a new scandal appearing in Congress, in state-owned companies, in the Federal Chamber, in state assemblies and in city councils.

Unlike other, more advanced countries, where prisoners go to jail, whether they are poor, rich or millionaires, no matter what the crime is, petty, simple or heinous. In Brazil it's different.

Out there, the accused, even without being convicted, are shown to the public in handcuffs, filmed, photographed, with striped uniforms and even a ball on their feet. Convicted, they receive harsh sentences and serve them all: 10, 20, 40 years, life imprisonment and even the death penalty. Be they artists, businessmen, politicians, young people or children. How envious we are.

Here you can't punish rigorously, the Human Rights Commission is vigilant, never in favor of the victims, prisoners are guaranteed privileges, beds, food, cell phones, television, intimate visits, prison aid, benefits that many honest and free citizens don't have.

Even when sentences are announced, there is deception in the judiciary. Heinous crimes, massacres, when the perpetrators are tried and convicted, judges usually hand down sentences of 100, 200 and even 400 years, even though our Penal Code does not allow any prisoner to spend more than 30 years behind bars.

But the people don't know this and believe what they hear.

With the benefits of sentence progression, then, good behavior, work and study, the majority of those sentenced to the maximum sentence do not spend 10 years in a closed regime.

And during this time of imprisonment, the prisoner receives financial aid, the government provides for his family, and if he works, wants to study, even reads books in his cell, the sentence is reduced further, the convict quickly gains supervised freedom, he can even rob during the day and return to jail at night.

If you have a university degree, even better, it guarantees you a special cell and lots of perks.

Tough luck for those who didn't study.

Justice doesn't work here in Brazil, impunity reigns supreme. Bandits have perks, cell phones, women and barbecues in prisons. Maximum security is a joke, criminals run crime from inside their cells, steal, rob and kill to order, with the help of lawyers and jailers and relatives.

There is a parallel government in the country.

There are millions of cases on hold, awaiting judgment, in the queue, with no expectation of another 10 or 20 years, if they don't expire. There are neighbor disputes, family disputes, traffic accidents, murders, extradition, chicken thefts. Everything goes through several instances, courts, juries and trials, appeals, reviews, annulments, impediments and then to the Supreme Court. Which forgets, shelves, returns, annuls, reduces the penalty, frees, strengthens impunity.

STF judges almost exchange punches in the Supreme Court, chatting like teenagers in class, the subject is personal issues, vanities, judgments that are put off until later. What's important is that they're in the media, broadcast live on TV, it's popular, maybe tomorrow they'll get a position in Congress, a deputy, a senator, a minister of some kind, maybe President of the Republic?

A minister who decides to work, wants to be fair and impartial in his judgments, condemns criminals without looking at their face, power or party, receives strong pressure, death threats, ends up asking for retirement 10 years early.

The business in the judiciary is to pretend, or to do nothing at all. Salaries for the good guys are guaranteed, jobs aren't in danger, pensions are too, so it's better not to change anything, leave it as it is, and bad luck for those waiting in line for justice that never comes.

Isn't the Supreme Court the end of the line?

It is difficult for ordinary citizens to understand how the Brazilian judiciary works. There are so many appeals that any litigation takes years for a final and unappealable decision. And everything reaches the Supreme Court. Whether it's a criminal case, a labor case, a political case or even a residential condominium charge that was dismissed at first instance.

If the appellant is wealthy, a successful businessman, has a lot of money and prominence on the social scene, is a prestigious politician, good lawyers will make the process move at a breakneck pace, using injunctions, embargoes and loopholes that poorly drafted laws allow.

If, however, the litigant is poor, without any financial resources, he runs the risk of having his case closed at the first hearing, and being ordered to pay his debt or his offense immediately.

Isn't the Supreme Court the final instance for any case that reaches it after years of appeals and embargoes? It should be, but it isn't. I learned this the other day during the Mensaleiros trial. In the Supreme Court, there are also appeals called "embargatórios", "infringentes" and so on, which give the condemned another chance to seek to invalidate the decision that should be the last.

The Mensalão trial explains everything. After more than nine years, various legal tricks, politicians were tried and convicted by the Supreme Court, all broadcast on TV in real time and followed with special interest by the population.

The long-awaited sentence came, applauded by some, criticized by others. There were politicians who received four, 10 and 15 years in prison, Marcos Valério, the head, got 40 years in jail. Months passed, appeals came in, and ordinary citizens were generally disappointed to discover that even there, in the Supreme Court, there are chicanery, loopholes, and the power of the condemned and their lawyers.

And what has happened? Many of those already convicted in the STF's plenary session have had their sentences reviewed, reduced and transformed into semi-open and open regimes, and are already free, even having their assets blocked by those who received 40 years in prison. By the same judges who sentenced them.

Can you believe in justice like that?

The Federal Supreme Court should exist to judge and give the final word only on issues of national interest, to settle doubts about constitutional articles and laws, to create jurisprudence on controversial issues, to decide on the installation of plebiscites and reforms to the Constitution.

Never judge whether a chicken thief should remain in prison.

Final decisions on civil or criminal appeals should end up in the STJ-Supreme Court of Justice.

Police arrest, Justice releases:

Faced with doubt, uncertainty and discredit, questions remain. Why do the courts release so many people whom the police arrest? Could it be that the evidence presented is always fragile and unsupported? If this is true, wouldn't it be prudent to investigate further, gather more evidence, more concrete proof before denouncing someone and even arresting them?

Wouldn't it be more sensible for the Public Prosecutor's Office or the police, whether state or federal, to collect all the accusatory material against someone quietly, analyze the evidence and documents, and then present them to the courts and ask for the arrest of the accused?

And for judges, wouldn't it be more logical and fair to create jurisprudence, demand and accept well-drafted complaints and avoid granting habeas corpus in a vulgar way? It would avoid vexations and confrontations and would not leave the population with the feeling of incompetence and impunity that the "arrest and release" system offers.

If there aren't enough places in jail for all the prisoners, the problem shouldn't lie with the judges, but with the Ministry of Justice, with the government authorities, which should turn to building or outsourcing new prisons.

Reducing the Penal Age:

Surveys carried out among the population to find out what people think about reducing the age of majority in Brazil were absolute: 93% are in favor of lowering the penal age to at least 16. It's a national consensus.

Could it be that the Constitution forbids it, that judges don't want to or don't have the sensitivity to judge and punish case by case, according to their conscience, without being bound by the coldness of the laws?

We must punish with the same rigor and penalty as an adult, a confessed minor murderer, no matter what age he or she is, when the crime committed by him or her involves death, robbery or a futile motive.

Three years, as it is today, is too little for heinous crimes committed by minors. And because of the lack of structure for re-education, when this young person gets out, he'll be a monster, more dangerous to society.

Scholars and experts on the subject say that when minors steal, rob and kill, it's our fault, society's fault, the moral values we've lost and others we've built. Consumerism is one of them. We know that. Just as we know that nothing is going to change as quickly as we want.

Unless we invest heavily in education. Which only gains importance in political promises.

The government has nothing but excuses, it says it has no money for schools, it doesn't change anything. It turns a blind eye to the problem, demonstrates incompetence, raises taxes. But where's the money?

We can't wait any longer, we can't stay locked up at home, afraid to go out into the streets, afraid of the bandits killing us. We need to react.

No more hearing the same speeches: Police arrest, Justice releases, Statute guarantees, minors have rights, they can't be arrested, only apprehended. We need to resolve this impasse, change the penal age to 16. At that age, young people already have a conscience, they know what they want and what they do. They can vote if they want to, get married, and many are already parents.

It would be good if judges, politicians and other public authorities could experience for a few moments the drama of loss and the suffering of impunity that someone who is a victim of violence by an underage offender goes through. Perhaps, suffering the same pain, the authorities will stop making useless speeches and be more rigorous in punishing criminals, whether they are adults or minors?

Changes can be made if you wish. Here's a proposal:

Why don't the Armed Forces, instead of selecting and forcing young people from all walks of life to do compulsory military service every year, which is almost always uninteresting for most of them, start housing the juvenile offenders who are dumped and abandoned in the Recovery Centers, the former FEBEMs throughout the country?

If every young person who committed crimes went to an Army, Navy or Air Force unit and stayed there for a year studying, working, learning a trade and receiving military discipline, they would probably come out recovered and with a chance of a better future.

Violence is a public calamity:

If a lot of rain, landslides, floods and a few deaths are grounds for declaring a Public Calamity, why are a lot of assaults, robberies, kidnappings, buses set on fire, ATM explosions and murders, all out of control, not also considered a Public Calamity?

Let's go, mayors of all Brazilian cities, make use of the right to declare a situation of Public Calamity in your cities, in view of the escalation of violence.

Take a fresh look at Article 136 of the Brazilian Constitution, which states that Public Calamity is defined as "misfortune, disgrace, disaster resulting from human action or from a fact of nature and which produces negative consequences for a society".

We know that the violence in big cities, which torments and causes panic among citizens, comes from the human or inhuman action of bandits and criminals, which characterizes misfortune, misfortune, and can also be considered a Public Calamity. All the government authorities have to do is say so.

The police have already shown that they are incapable of stopping this wave of crime and of providing people with the slightest security, whether on the streets, at work or in their homes. And security or the lack of it has already become a paranoia among Brazilians and is causing negative consequences in society.

Because of the violence, there are people with all kinds of traumas, paralyzed by fear, who no longer leave the house, stop working or retire early.

Psychologists and psychoanalysts can tell you that.

The truth is that if the violence isn't contained, if it doesn't stay at bearable levels, the people will soon start demanding the death penalty in the country.

Or even take the law into their own hands.

Who doesn't care about the death penalty?

To bandits and criminals, of course!

I have no problem with the death penalty in Brazil. I'm honest, hard-working and I don't intend to rob or kill anyone. Just like you, who are reading this now.

The death penalty is of no interest to some intellectuals and human rights personnel. This is an important body that should be on the side of minorities, the wronged, the ideologically and politically persecuted. And not in defense of barbaric criminals, young or old.

Life imprisonment and the death penalty are also of no interest to religious organizations, because they take life, and according to them, they distort the teachings of Christ, which preach respect for life and condemn death. Although bandits and criminals don't think and act like that.

Society is clamoring for a reduction in the age of criminal responsibility to 14, 15, or at least 16, and a change from three years' imprisonment for teenage criminals to eight or ten years.

Public opinion polls are revealing across the country that no one accepts the impunity and privileges given to minors who commit robberies with fatalities. Children, young people and adults need to regain their fear and respect for justice.

There is a lot of resistance, the authorities don't want to listen to society's pleas, they want to appear advanced, modern and cover up their incompetence. They prefer to rely on the articles of the Childhood and Adolescence Statute, which give children and young people various rights and few duties, obligations or penalties.

Will it take a young offender robbing and killing a political figurehead or one of his family members for them to change their minds?

No one in their right mind wants to punish children and adolescents for no reason, to deprive them of their fundamental rights, including childhood, education and inclusion in society. However, while the state does not structure itself to provide ideal conditions for young people and adolescents, with schools, leisure and work, it is necessary to protect good citizens, honorable families, by rigorously punishing those who decide to break the law, commit crimes and murder.

This is the case in the United States and in most European countries. There are cases of 12-year-olds serving life sentences and others awaiting the death penalty.

What we can't do is continue to listen to hypocritical speeches from our rulers, politicians, judges and religious leaders, trying to cover up their incompetence, turning a blind eye to the gratuitous violence that is rampant in the cities, with robberies and killings, almost all of which are participated in or commanded by minors under the age of 18, boys and girls, some as young as 10.

It is no longer acceptable for confessed murderers who have been clearly identified by images and hard evidence to be arrested and immediately released on writs of habeas corpus, procedures that were widely used and acceptable during the military dictatorship to guarantee civil rights and curb arrests, excesses and torture against people who were simply fighting against the regime. Such privileges for common criminals cannot be justified.

Why not the death penalty in Brazil? More developed countries have life imprisonment and the death penalty. In the United States, our main partner, an evolved nation and the main address of our dreams, of the 51 states of the federation, 33 still use the maximum penalty to punish crimes involving death. There are various methods of execution: sometimes by electric chair, gas chamber, lethal injection, hanging and firing squad. And for those who escape summary execution, almost all states impose life imprisonment on the condemned.

You can't agree with the discourse that it's against God's law, that no one can take the life of their fellow man. But can criminals? Ask anyone who has been the victim of a kidnapping, had their house invaded, spent the night in the hands of bandits or had their wife or child cowardly killed in a robbery because of a pair of sneakers or because they didn't have more than 30 reais, what they think of the death penalty or life imprisonment? However religious they may be, I doubt that at this time they are not in favor of the death penalty.

Most important of all is the educational lesson that a strict law can bring to those who rob, steal and needlessly kill. Knowing how strict the laws are, bandits start to think that by acting violently, robbing and killing, when they are arrested, they can be sentenced to death. It's the old Talion Law, an eye for an eye, a tooth for a tooth, which was important and beneficial in a prehistoric era of humanity, when men acted like savages. Just like the bandits of Brazilian reality.

During the Military Dictatorship in Brazil, we already had the death penalty for political terrorists, many of whom are now sheltering in power, and who were condemned at the time for having a goal, a flag, an ideology. Why not adopt the death penalty now, against bandits who have no flag, no ideology, who kill for nothing, for no reason?

They'll say: it's not politically correct.

If the President of the Republic doesn't want to heed the calls of parliamentarians who have their own interests, she should listen to the demands of the people and use her powers to invoke National Security and issue a decree instituting the death penalty in Brazil for a fixed period of time, until violence and crime rates reach humanly bearable levels.

It may even be that, with the threat of the death penalty, homicide and robbery crimes will decrease considerably and the state won't need to execute anyone. As, fortunately, it didn't execute any opponents of the military regime.

Zero Tolerance Law:

Why can't Zero Tolerance be applied in Brazil, as Mayor Rudolph Giuliani did in New York in the 1990s? It was a success! The city was violent, many muggings, robberies and killings frightened the city's residents. The bandits were daring, showing no fear of the police or of justice. It was like now in Brazil: bandits were arrested and then released and went on to commit new crimes. Both adults and teenagers. And corruption was prevalent, even affecting the police.

The then mayor, Giuliani, courageously implemented a series of strict measures to curb the escalating violence. He carried out a sweep of the police force, sacked several officers considered to be corrupt, and started arresting and imprisoning anyone who was committing any kind of crime. From simple robberies to homicides. And he remained unyielding. He would arrest adults and teenagers, take them to the judges on duty, who, given the evidence, would set bail on the spot, which was always high, and the sentences to be served.

The police and the justice system have regained their credibility.

Crime has not stopped, but today, violence in New York is contained, there are no acts of vandalism, depredations and riots in the city, and robberies and homicides have fallen to insignificant levels and are not even noticed by the population. All it took was political will and the determination of one authority for everything to change. For the better.

And why shouldn't such a plan be adopted here in Brazil? The authorities would certainly have the full support of the population, with positive rates never seen in any previous proposal.

All the courts have to do is make it clear and publicize it in institutional campaigns that from now on, anyone who commits any crime, be it graffiti, vandalism, small or large thefts, robberies, ATM explosions, kidnappings and murders, will be immediately arrested, taken to a judge on duty, pay a very high bail if it's a small crime, and be detained in a closed regime if it's a heavy crime, until their case is definitively judged.

If the offender is a minor, the treatment will be the same. They will be detained, sent to a rehabilitation institution, an educational institution, a reformatory, and depending on the crime, the sentence could be an alternative, or many years in prison under a closed regime. And as a preventative measure, minors wandering the streets during school hours will be picked up, taken home and their parents held responsible.

There won't be enough jails for so many people who will be arrested, many will say. Let's build as many jails as necessary. They don't have to be big prisons. They can be small establishments, with a maximum capacity of 100 prisoners, one in each neighborhood of the big cities. And they can be outsourced, built and run by private companies. Only controlled by governments. They are cheaper and more efficient.

While violence increases, questions circulate and indignation spreads, the police come to the media and do their marketing saying that patrols have been increased, more vehicles are on the streets, that the indices show that assaults, robberies and murders are decreasing.

People don't see it that way.

The country's jails and prisons are overcrowded with prisoners who have committed all kinds of crimes. From those who are murderers, bank robbers, drug dealers, to those who have committed petty crimes such as robbery and theft, without physical violence. All occupying space and generating costs, for one, five, ten or even twenty years in prison.

According to recent statistics, each criminal in jail costs the state 2,900 reais a month in tax money. The majority of Brazilian workers don't even come close to receiving this amount every month.

If justice is rigorous and immediate in punishing crimes, violence will certainly decrease.

There are many proposals. You just have to be willing to put them into practice. Here's one more:

Wild West Project:

Project Wild West is a reference to the Law Enforcement Officers of the United States of America, the well-known sheriffs and deputies who arrested and enforced the laws in their own way in the towns of the Old West.

Some of the habits and procedures of that time, almost 200 years ago, could still be applied in Brazil to prevent and instantly punish the perpetrators of various crimes.

The proposal is as simple as it is easy to implement:

A few years ago, more precisely on May 24, 2000, the CONSEP-Community Council for Public Safety was created in Minas Gerais. Today, there are already several of them spread across various neighborhoods in Belo Horizonte and cities in Minas Gerais.

As stated in their statutes, the main function of CONSEPs is to bring together community leaders, police authorities and other public bodies directly or indirectly linked to public safety, in order to discuss and adopt practical measures that result in improving the quality of life of communities, especially those that are more exposed to risk factors that interfere with human dignity.

Fourteen years after its creation, we know that few councils are functioning as expected, and the reasons range from the lack of availability of people, the lack of autonomy of CONSEPs, to the lack of interest and disbelief of the population with regard to security policies. Meanwhile, violence is on the rise.

What would the proposal look like?

First: to expand the CONSEPs (Community Public Safety Councils) to all the neighborhoods of Belo Horizonte. These CONSEPs would be made up of representatives of religious organizations in the neighborhood, who could be priests, pastors; presidents of community associations, principals of municipal and private schools, shopkeepers.

Secondly, the people summoned to work for CONSEP would be volunteers, receiving at most an incentive, which could be an exemption from paying the IPTU (property tax) or giving them a transport voucher while they were working.

Thirdly, people would be hired every two years, through elections in the community, when there was more than one volunteer, and without any employment ties.

Fourth: CONSEP would operate in its own premises, either owned or rented by the municipality, or it could be attached to a health center already operating in the neighborhood.

Fifth: these CONSEP offices in each neighborhood could add various services of interest to the community, such as
* Health center
* Police station
* INSS office
* Procon Unit
* Conciliation Board
* ATMs.

The health center and police station would operate 24 hours a day, meeting the demands of the local community.

INSS Office, Procon Unit, Conciliation Board, during business hours, from 7 a.m. to 7 p.m., Monday to Friday.

ATMs would be open from 7 a.m. to 10 p.m. daily.

Sixth: Jails. To relieve the overcrowded prisons, the city or state could build small jails in the public areas along the East West Expressway, for example, next to and under the viaducts, to house individuals who commit petty crimes such as assaults, robberies and other crimes that don't result in homicides. These jails would be small but secure, built with concrete walls and steel floors and would hold a maximum of 50 prisoners each.

Seventh: Provisional cells. In the style of Western films, these could be part of the services attached to the Police Station in each neighborhood, cells for the temporary detention of a maximum of four people from the community who commit minor crimes, such as theft, dragnetting, contempt, fights, aggression, drug possession, etc.

Before being taken to provisional detention, these offenders would go through the Conciliation Board, where they could make an agreement, pay bail, be identified and released. If there are no agreements or bail payments, and depending on the offense, the offenders would be detained in cells for a maximum of 48 hours, as a punishment, and if the infractions are minor, these people would be released and legal proceedings would be opened against them.

The whole procedure would be monitored by a group of citizens of proven integrity, members of the CONSEPs, chosen from among representatives of the Church, Education, the Community Association and the Judiciary, represented by lawyers or law trainees.

Eighth: Bail. All people who committed so-called petty crimes would have to pay a bail or fine, small amounts of money stipulated in a table of offenses. As happens in traffic charges and in the financial system, where interest, fines and fees are charged on late payments for various private and public services.

And these bails and fines would go towards maintaining the CONSEPs in each neighborhood.

With the implementation in the judiciary of the practices adopted by traffic laws, which punish offenders almost instantaneously with monetary fines that vary according to the seriousness of the infractions committed, this simplistic solution could greatly reduce overcrowding in the prison system.

Everyone knows that in order to have educational value, no matter how minor the infraction or crime committed by someone, the correction, warning or punishment has to happen immediately, as soon as the fact occurs. This is how good parents educate their children.

The Brazilian justice system could adopt this procedure of fines and points for people who commit minor offenses, instead of simply seizing them, or arresting them, opening criminal proceedings, which take years to complete and then putting the convicts in prisons that are already overcrowded.

Someone once said that the pocket is the part of the human being that hurts the most.

All it would take is for the courts to draw up a list of minor offenses and set a financial amount for each one as a fine, adding a number of negative points for each offense, which would be entered in the offenders' records. Whenever a person accumulated a certain number of points on their record, criminal proceedings would be opened against them, which, once judged, could result in conditional imprisonment, monitored by electronic anklets.

A good city is not one where even the poor drive, but one where even the rich use public transport. Such cities are not a hippie delusion. They already exist.
(Enrique Peñalosa, former mayor of Bogotá)

URBAN MOBILITY

How precarious public transportation is:

Year in, year out, Carnival, Holy Week, end-of-year parties, school holidays, recesses, and the problem of people's mobility continues to be a torment. Crowded airports, poor road transportation, bad and dangerous roads, accidents and deaths are all part of Brazilians' journeys. This is the scenario for those who need to use airports, state and federal roads and highways.

The same is true of public transport in the capitals and cities of the metropolitan regions. This chaos is repeated daily for those who use private cars, take buses or use the only metro line, such as the one in the city of Belo Horizonte. Unlike Rio de Janeiro and São Paulo, there are no other suburban train branches or auxiliary lines for passenger transportation.

Disrespectful to users.

There are lots of promises, they always appear in the media, if there are elections coming up the better, but projects are never carried out. It's a cynical game of push and shove between government bodies and entities. Total incompetence. City halls on one side, state and federal governments on the other. One says it has released funds, the other claims not to know where the money is, the other has no projects ready.

This is what is happening with the BR 381 in Minas Gerais, the Ring Road in Belo Horizonte, the metro and passenger trains all over Brazil. Promised for years, neglected, abandoned.

In Minas Gerais alone, President Dilma came several times during her first term to announce and release billions of reais in funding for urban mobility projects. To this day, four years later, no projects have appeared, only studies, Metro Minas has issued a confusing tender for the BH metro, which has not attracted any interested parties, BR 381 and the Ring Road continue in the same way. Causing accidents and deaths all the time.

Is it a lie, money never got here, or incompetence on the part of the governors and mayors, who don't have projects, don't know how to execute them?

In 2012, the state government promised to resume passenger trains on the Sete Lagoas, Betim, Contagem stretch, but nothing practical has happened so far. The city halls of Contagem and Betim announced an agreement with FCA, the freight transportation concessionaire, which promised a passenger train linking the two cities to the Eldorado metro station. No one is reporting it.

Until when will the public authorities responsible for mass transportation stop playing games with the people, turning a blind eye to the suffering of those who, in order to survive, have to use a precarious commuting service, knowing that funds exist and are not being applied to the expansion of metro lines and the reactivation of kilometers of idle railway sidings in the capital and neighboring cities?

The issue of urban mobility has become a major concern for Brazilian citizens. It is the topic that dominates the main debates on the country's radio and television programs. Interest has even surpassed discussions on health, education and public safety.

And the people have every reason to be dissatisfied.

Public transport in Brazil is literally mass transportation. A mass of maneuvering, since, innocently, we all travel to the slaughterhouse every day, like oxen, we are taken in by the talk of politicians, we believe in promises that are never fulfilled.

We are maneuvered, humiliated, treated like cattle going to the slaughterhouse, with no reaction. You only have to get on a public transport vehicle in the big cities, or on the suburban trains or subway cars to feel the drama, the suffering of those who have no alternative means of getting around.

Squeezed like sardines in a can, men, women, children and the elderly travel for hours without any comfort or safety. Women, then, suffer the most from sexual abuse by men who take advantage of the squeeze. And if they complain, they run the risk of being physically assaulted.

It's bankrupt public transport.

Rail transportation:

Nobody understands the reasons why many municipal, state and federal governments that have democratically passed through our country insist so much on the road model for transporting cargo and passengers.

It is well known that building roads and keeping them in a good state of repair is very expensive, and even with the privatization of some highways, demand is high and accidents are repeated in intensity every year, as the number of vehicles on the road is increasing.

Throughout the civilized world, railroads have a prominent place in freight and passenger transport. They are efficient, fast, comfortable, carry more people and more cargo at the same time. And the risks of accidents and deaths are almost zero.

In major cities around the world, the high-speed metro system is of high quality, with several branches leading to various points, which is why it is widely used.

In Brazil, both passenger and freight transportation by rail, as well as subways, are neglected in official planning and receive little funding. With the exception of the cities of Rio de Janeiro and São Paulo, which have a good rail network in use, and a reasonable subway system, albeit shrouded in corruption and embezzlement, no other Brazilian city has even an efficient subway that serves the interests of passengers well.

Road freight transportation is chaotic. Most highways are narrow, two lanes only, full of potholes and no safety for drivers, who are forced to travel day and night without stopping, due to the lack of support points on the highways. And there has been a law in force for more than a year that obliges drivers to rest every four hours when driving their trucks.

It only works on paper.

Do you know why? They forgot to provide the roads with infrastructure, build shelters, dormitories, toilets and offer minimum safety to drivers.

The Belo Horizonte metro is more than 40 years in the making. And it only has a 28 km line, which precariously serves just over 170,000 passengers a day, when the population is already approaching three million. Priority lines, such as the one to Barreiro, have been abandoned for years and two others, from Savassi and Centro to Pampulha, are just political promises.

A lot of money has already been earmarked for the BH metro in recent years. At least on paper and in politicians' speeches. We have several abandoned railway sidings in the capital and neighboring cities that could be reactivated and passenger trains built on them to relieve the intense flow of vehicles and buses on our streets and avenues.

The government prefers to insist on outdated road solutions, such as the BRT (Bus Rapid Transit), now renamed MOVE (articulated bus), promising other lines for the Via Expressa Leste Oeste and the already strangled Av.Amazonas road corridor.   Hard to understand.

I don't want to be frivolous or accuse anyone, but I suspect that there is strong pressure from the owners and concessionaires of bus lines to hinder investment in new subway lines, the monorail and the idle rail network, which could help and connect cities near Belo Horizonte.

Why do the works always promised for Urban Mobility in Belo Horizonte and neighboring cities never get off the ground?

Why is it that two or three times a year the President of the Republic comes to Minas and announces the allocation of funds for the subway, the Ring Road and BR 381 and the work never happens?

Why is there no interest on the part of municipal and state authorities in immediately reactivating suburban passenger trains to relieve the enormous congestion on the roads?

Why doesn't anyone demand that rail freight concessionaires such as FCA, MRS and VALE fulfill their contractual obligation to offer passenger trains or allow outsourced companies to do so?

Why can't an idle railway branch line that is still in good condition between Gameleira Station and Barreiro be used immediately to help transport passengers, by putting a few wagons pulled by a diesel-powered machine there to run at least in the mornings and afternoons?

Why, in Belo Horizonte, does City Hall insist on the idea of an underground subway line linking the city center to Savassi, when it could enter into a public-private partnership with a company in the capital that already has a project ready to implement a much cheaper monorail system in a short time, linking Belvedere to the center, Pampulha, the Administrative City and Confins Airport?

Why do thousands of people leave their homes, face hours of traffic jams and queues to watch a soccer match, take to the streets to protest against or in favor of homosexual marriage, participate in the Gay Parade and are unable to gather in a public square to demand that the authorities carry out immediate work to solve mass transportation in Belo Horizonte and neighboring cities?

Why is that?

Even Freud can't explain it.

Reactivation of railway sidings:

Government in, government out and the promises of investment in subways are repeated in speeches and don't appear in practice. The excuses are always the same: the costs are high and there are no funds available in the National Treasury. But they are there to be misappropriated and misused in ghost works or works that are never finished. And there are many examples of this in various parts of the country.

The transportation situation in Brazil is chaotic. In the air, there are few routes and constant and long flight delays. Sea freight doesn't seem to work very well and river transportation is hardly used at all. All the weight and flow of cargo and tourist travel is carried out on Brazil's highways, which are of very poor quality, with single lanes, full of curves, accidents and thousands of deaths. More than many wars between peoples and countries.

Nobody talks about the rail options. There is a contempt for the subject. If a curious person mentions the train, someone is quick to say that there are no more tracks and that replacing the network is too expensive. I doubt it. There must be strong opposing interests, people from the road sector, politicians and businessmen who don't want to change the failed model.

Which makes money for many.

Even if you spend more on a railroad than on building or widening a road, the benefits and advantages of a train are infinitely greater. Railroads last a long time, require little maintenance and there are almost no accidents or fatalities. And there are other advantages not yet mentioned. These few advantages alone would be enough to invest heavily in rail transport.

Are we going to demand answers?

Wasn't it Vale, our largest mining company in the world, that put an end to passenger transportation by train? Wasn't it Vale that took over most of Brazil's railroad stretches, especially in Minas Gerais, to transport ore to the large freighters anchored in ports along the Brazilian coast? Doesn't it spend millions on advertising to say that it is socially responsible, that it protects the environment?

Why not force Vale by law to set aside a percentage of its profits to build a new passenger rail network in Brazil? It would be an objective way of giving back to the people for the wealth it takes for free from Brazilian soil and sends abroad at a bargain price. But it makes a profit. Vale itself could build and buy the trains and manage the system. All it needs to do is create a subsidiary.

How nice it would be to return to the old, much-needed stretches of railroad linking metropolitan cities to Belo Horizonte. They are still there, owned by Vale. In the cities of Nova Lima, Raposos, Sabará. Lagoa Santa, Pedro Leopoldo - Sarzedo, Betim-Divinópolis, Sete Lagoas, Ceasa- Barreiro, Cidade Industrial. You just have to want it, have sensitivity and political will. Without demagoguery.

The train is essential for connecting cities to others, the metro is irreplaceable for transporting and moving passengers quickly, but the monorail, transport on rails in the heights, does away with intersections on the ground, puts an end to crossings and intersections of streets and avenues, and is therefore quieter and faster. And it costs less to build.

No need for expropriation.

And why are they ignoring the monorail?

Although the monorail, the subway suspended on pillars, has been proven to be the best and cheapest transportation system for the city of Belo Horizonte, we don't hear the municipal and state authorities committing to its implementation. What we do hear is the mayor of Belo Horizonte reaffirming his willingness to build an underground subway line linking the center of the capital to Savassi. This is an expensive and technically unfeasible project because of the disruption it will cause.

There is no sensibility among politicians and other municipal and state authorities to quickly solve the problems of mass transportation in large cities, especially Belo Horizonte and neighboring cities, where congestion is already close to chaos.

Strangely, no one is showing any interest in reactivating the railroad branches that could connect several cities around Belo Horizonte and they don't even report on the studies paid for and completed years ago by a Spanish consortium, which suggests the implementation of a monorail connecting the subway to Belvedere and Lagoinha station to Confins airport, passing through Pampulha.

Stubbornly, the mayors of the metropolitan region insist on investing in road transport, public buses and giving priority to private vehicles. And another mayor, here in Belo Horizonte, who wants to appear smarter, is drilling into the capital's soil to find out how far and how expensive the metro can be underground.

And we, the citizens who are mistreated and humiliated by public transport, do nothing to demand improvements.

So we deserve all this suffering.

DNIT's make-believe:

People are tired of hearing "I don't know", "we're preparing the project", "the tender will be in 90 days", "the work will start next year", or even worse: "the speed cameras have been deactivated for two years due to legal action". These are the answers heard and repeated every time DNIT officials are asked about measures to resolve the accidents and deaths on the Ring Road and BR 381, to Vitória.

Lack of creativity and responsibility.

There are no objective and immediate proposals from the responsible authorities. From the interviews with DNIT representatives, it is clear that the agency has neither the autonomy nor the competence to solve anything, that everything comes from above, more precisely from the political will of Brasilia. The rest is hot air.

From what it does and fails to do, the conclusion is that DNIT shouldn't even exist. It has become nothing more than a place for jobs. It is clear that there is no autonomy or competence in DNIT, which leads us to conclude that whether this body exists or not, things remain the way they are.

The country's roads are in terrible condition. Everyone knows it, the press publicizes it, warns and denounces the potholes, the dangers and the neglect of the authorities.

Tragedies repeat themselves.

Every weekend, accidents and deaths multiply. Entire families are lost due to the recklessness of drivers and the need to dodge potholes.

If it weren't enough that the Urban Civil War is already underway, with people being mugged and killed for any reason, people are dying on the highways because of the curves and potholes. It's the fatality foretold, with the perpetrator identified: the Federal Government! And nobody does anything, they don't react. They just complain in isolation.

BH's Ring Road, a sad example:

Year in, year out and no work is carried out on the Belo Horizonte Ring Road.

This 27-kilometer road, within the urban area of the capital of Minas Gerais, is used by around 120,000 vehicles a day, including cars, buses, trucks and trailers.

I no longer believe in speeches and promises. I'm in favour of mobilizing people, peaceful demonstrations and protests. That's why I'm asking questions:

- Why is no workers' organization taking the initiative to lead a protest movement and stop the Ring Road?

- Where is the MG Trade Association, the OAB, the CDL, FIEMG, the bus workers' unions and even the Catholic, Protestant and Evangelical churches that aren't mobilizing and taking a stand?

After all, what is the point of these organizations, associations and churches that regularly and unforgivingly collect monthly fees, annuities and tithes from their members and faithful? If they really are defenders of quality of life, work and people's physical and spiritual well-being, they should be the first to take the lead in a popular and peaceful demonstration to demand that the authorities start work on the Ring Road immediately.

All it would take is for a union, an association or any organization representing a large number of workers or businesspeople to go public and call on their members to demonstrate. It would be enough for everyone to get together once a week on a stretch of the Ring Road, close it and bring traffic to a standstill for an hour, and the widening and modernization work would certainly begin immediately.

It's just not possible for a handful of indignant and courageous people like me, you and a few others who read me to do this on their own. We'll certainly be beaten up by the police and arrested for inciting public disorder.
More questions:

- Why aren't the transport companies, associations, truck drivers, workers' organizations and business owners in the road sector, who allege losses, mobilizing?

- Why, after so many accusations and tragedies, do organizations like FIEMG and CNT, which claim to represent industries and transport companies, not take effective initiatives to demand immediate action from the government?

- Why don't the municipal and state governments declare a State of Emergency on the Ring Road and BR 381 to force the federal government to release sufficient funds and allow work to begin immediately without a tender?

Part of the blame lies with the politicians, who do nothing. The other, bigger part, is ours, because we only complain, we don't react.

Is flying only for birds?

To understand Brazilian air transportation, you have to literally get off the ground and fly. Go through the air. It is completely disorganized, incompetent, lacking in professionalism and, above all, respect for users. The country has never seen such anarchy in the air and on the ground since Santos-Dumont invented the 14 Bis.

Brazilian airports, considered international, cannot be compared to those in the world's major capitals. It's sad when we leave Brazil, from Guarulhos, the best airport here, and get off in any city in the United States or Europe. Even small cities there have airports and boarding and disembarking infrastructure that are superior to ours.

Unacceptable and shameful.

What is quite strange and worrying is the attitude of the bodies that take care of aviation in Brazil, such as ANAC, the regulatory agency, Infraero, the Air Force, the Ministry of Defense, the Presidency of the Republic, and especially the companies in the sector. No one really cares about passengers, customers of aviation businesses and, above all, citizens.

Is commercial passenger transportation not a profitable business for companies? Does it only make a loss? It doesn't seem to be worth it, since their customers, the passengers, are ignored and don't receive dignified, humane treatment at Brazilian airports.

Children, the elderly and the disabled are mistreated. Entire families are literally thrown to the ground. Flights are canceled, others delayed by several hours, without any convincing explanation. Each body transfers responsibility to the other and no one solves or decides anything.

The government should have already threatened to intervene, nationalize companies along the lines of authoritarianism, or propose deregulating the sector so that foreign companies could enter, in the neoliberal style.
Then the crisis would be over in an instant!

We can't say that there is a monopoly in the sector, but there is a cartel. There are practically two companies that dominate national air traffic. Gol and Tam. The third, Azul, is small and unable to compete with anything.

With only two companies, the prices are high and almost the same and the quality and punctuality of the flights are the worst possible. On top of that, there's the terrible structure of Brazil's main airports.

The solution is for all workers to unite, hold protests and take to the streets to demand greater investment in Brazilian aviation and public transport.

Corrupt tenders:

Society demands construction work, roads, railroads, subways, businessmen say they can do it, the government comes along, calls the press, announces billions in funding, no project appears, nothing gets off the ground, the work doesn't get done.

Meetings, seminars, workshops and lectures are repeated in bodies and trade associations to discuss the issue. Presidents, superintendents, directors of state-owned companies are invited, some attend, talk, clarify nothing, just promise like politicians, present no projects, only proposals, there is no centrality in decisions.

Why don't they build infrastructure the way they build apartment buildings? The entrepreneur has the land, makes a construction project, gets it approved by the relevant bodies, goes to the financing agent, Caixa, Banco do Brasil, private banks, asks for a loan, gives guarantees, gets a loan and pays it off in 20, 30 years.

The project is approved, the money comes in gradually, according to the progress of the work. Once everything is finished, the entrepreneur negotiates the units and pays the Agent with a grace period and reduced interest. The entrepreneur makes the profit, the government collects the taxes. Nobody complains and there is construction everywhere.

Public works could be like this. The government draws up a project, puts it out to tender, a company bids, wins, proves that it has the technical and financial capacity to take on the work, be it a subway line, a highway, a railway branch, a viaduct, a soccer stadium. It then calculates the costs of labor, materials, profit margin, completion time, incorporates forecast inflation, borrows the money from the government, takes on the risks, carries out the work, keeps the management and profits from the project and undertakes to pay for everything in 30, 50 years. With the income from the business itself.

Is it bad?

No, but nobody wants to work like that. Construction companies prefer the traditional, corrupt tenders, where prices and winners are agreed, the government delays paying, one company wins today, loses tomorrow, gets a subcontractor, always takes advantage and the values decided at the start of the work are changed and overpriced as the work goes on, and by the time it's finished, years have gone by. On many construction sites, companies go bankrupt and everything is abandoned halfway through, in the middle of the bush.

When living is a privilege, occupying is a right.
(No known author)

HOUSING

Is there housing for everyone?

Of course not! If it did, this would be Sweden, a first world, almost perfect country. But there could be less discrepancy, with some living very well, in luxury, and others in misery and abandonment. That's how it is in Brazil, a high housing deficit, lots of money to finance, the very popular Caixa Federal, which finances a lot, provides facilities for the rich, obstacles for the poor, low-income workers.

There is a lack of housing for a large part of the population. Housing policies only work at election time. They have no continuity. The government releases funds, gives incentives to construction companies, exempts them from taxes, registers thousands of interested parties, promises homes for everyone, but the majority are not served, they have no proven income, they earn from informal work.

Disappointment, premeditated deception, little gets off the ground, almost everything remains marketing. Huge projects are promised, billions are spent on soccer stadiums, the transposition of the São Francisco River never comes to an end, the PAC - Growth Acceleration Program becomes a pachyderm, it doesn't get off the ground. Money is earmarked, the press reports billions, nobody sees anything in the air, on land and at sea, nor does the government know where the money is or where it is going.

Neglect and incompetence are everywhere. Nobody monitors anything. It's all make-believe. Rubble is dumped every day on the streets and roads of the cities without any difficulty. Irregular constructions spring up every day on the sides of highways and the Ring Road. The Federal Police go back and forth and don't stop it. And there is a law at Dnit, the National Land Infrastructure Department, which says that it is forbidden to build in these places. Slums spring up overnight on the tops and bottoms of hills, on the banks of streams and rivers, and with the arrival of the rains they become tragedies.

It's good that everyone knows and becomes aware that there is land to build on, not always in city centers, and that it can house everyone who has nowhere to live. It's just a matter of unions and people organizing themselves, finding space, even on the outskirts, and demanding that the government provide the conditions to build a small but dignified shack.

It's wrong to invade private land.

Fortunes in funds disappear down the drain of corruption, people delude themselves and wait for houses, live on the streets, under bridges, build slums, generating violence, misery and corruption. Militias form to provide protection, promise shacks, take money from the needy. Soldiers turn into bandits, blend in with the good guys, take the place of drug dealers, and no one knows where to turn for help. The police or the bandits?

There isn't enough housing for all the families, the deficit is huge, we know that. There's empty public land, there's a lack of will and housing policy.

111

The same tragedy every year:

The end of the year and the beginning of the year, heavy rains as usual, the same scenario again. Floods, mudslides, landslides and deaths. And the sites of these tragedies are the same: hillsides, ravines, riverbanks.

And what is the government doing? No prevention. Only rescue, rapid, emergency care, after the fact. Like the police, who arrive after the crime has happened. The role of the fire department, no?

Why, instead of spending millions every year to help the victims of the rains, wouldn't it be more logical and less expensive for governments to remove these people from risk areas before tragedy strikes?

If the authorities wanted to, all they would have to do is plan each year to build a certain number of houses or apartments in a safe place, even if it's outside the city, and gradually move families out of these risky areas. And at the same time, isolate these areas, restore them, plant trees, ban and even imprison those who build or insist on returning.

From then on, you just have to plan honestly and for the long term, build housing, accommodate the homeless and gradually remove all the families who are on the hillsides and on the banks of streams and rivers, waiting for the next tragedy.

It takes years, but it has to be done.

Do you want to know who is responsible for these tragedies every year? The government! Municipal, state and federal. No one else. Not even those people, humble or not, poor or rich, who build their shacks or mansions in risky areas such as hills, mountains or the banks of streams and rivers.

It is the government authorities, at all levels, echelons and departments, civil and military, who are responsible for all these tragedies and deaths that happen because of the rains.
They are the ones who have never enforced the land use laws that all big cities have and which determine what, how and where residential and commercial properties can and should be built.

It is they, the Executive and the Legislative, who have never had the courage to create laws or issue strict decrees banning, fining and even imprisoning those who build in areas of risk or environmental preservation.

They are the mayors and councillors of the big cities who turn a blind eye and even accept bribes from businessmen and big construction companies to change urban occupation laws and allow speculators to build shopping malls and high-rise buildings in areas that were previously forbidden.

What happened near BH Shopping and in the Nova Lima region is an example of shameful corruption. They devastated and destroyed the environment. And nobody reacted. A few complained. In an environmentally protected area, Belo Horizonte's calling card, hundreds of buildings have been erected, mountains cut down and covered up.
Now even the south wind doesn't come that way.

It even seems that there are political interests in these tragedies being repeated every year. Like the drought industry in the Northeast, which has been going on for almost a century, receives huge sums of money every year, few people benefit and the problem never ends. But it enriches many entrepreneurs.

Today, Brazilians, as a rule, "amorcega", do everything by halves, screw over those who pay them, complain about their work and don't look at themselves in the mirror of competence.
(Luiz Carlos Prates, commentator for the RBS group in the south)

WORK AND EMPLOYMENT

There is work, there is a lack of jobs:

.

In most developed countries, employment is falling. Spain, Portugal and Greece, for example, have unemployment rates of over 25%. Mostly young people. In Brazil, for the time being, there are still a good number of jobs available, with vacancies to be filled. All of them, however, require qualifications.

Positions and jobs that used to be filled by people with few qualifications now require specific studies and knowledge. Waiters, salespeople, drivers, bill collectors and hotel porters now require high school and even college degrees, and many require a command of a foreign language. Even without explaining when and where it will be used.

There aren't jobs for everyone, some understand, resign themselves, become entrepreneurs, create micro-businesses, others seek informality in order to survive. Many delude themselves, join the queues for competitive exams, seek stability in the civil service, the government, Caixa, Banco do Brasil, the judiciary, the federal police. They spend years studying, sometimes funded by their family, they don't accumulate any practical experience, only theories, age arrives, no alternatives, disillusionment hits, their parents' house is the safe haven to face reality and the future.

With the recurring crises, companies are downsizing their staff, adding technology, and the traditional workforce is shrinking. It's obvious. Old professions disappear, new activities emerge, specialized professionals are slow to be trained.

The deficiencies in our education system are visible. Skills are not taught in schools, curricula are poorly designed, second languages are precarious, and there are few technical colleges. There are too many specialized jobs and not enough qualified workers.

The government only makes promises, fulfills little or nothing, deceives the poorest population with handouts, family grants, basic food baskets and food vouchers. It relieves and accommodates those who receive it, takes hope away from the disadvantaged, forms people who lack quality, respect and self-respect. Those who receive benefits from social programs are no longer individuals, nor are they citizens; they become animals, dependent on the support of others.

Employment as we know it, for many years in one place, with a formal contract, guaranteed rights, a fixed salary, paid on the 5th day of the month, is at an end. So say the experts. The economy is now globalized, all commerce is electronic, business is done over the internet, and in the near future, most work will be long-distance. The Home Office is already a reality. The company hires as a legal entity, pays a fixed monthly amount, stipulates daily tasks and commitments, the worker is self-employed, works from home, pays taxes and personal expenses. There are advantages and disadvantages.

There's plenty of work, no shortage, you just have to want it and specialize. Conventional employment, with rights and a formal contract, is shrinking, technologies are advancing, tasks are being outsourced, done remotely, at the contractor's own risk. It's a global trend.

And why not dare?

It's high time the government authorities were bolder and more creative, and presented society with a proposal that would revolutionize work in Brazil: something like the 36-hour week. Everyone working from Monday to Saturday, with six-hour shifts. There would be a considerable increase in vacancies in practically all sectors of the economy and less traffic congestion.

Why can't banks have longer opening hours, work during the day and at night? It would make life easier for businesses and many people. Public services could also work two or three six-hour shifts a day. It would reduce bureaucracy and serve the population more quickly and efficiently.

Imagine INSS offices open day and night for those who can only apply for pensions and other benefits at certain times? Can you imagine the DMV dealing with traffic accidents at any time, or health centers offering appointments in the morning, afternoon and evening for users of the public health system?

It seems like an impossible proposal to make a reality, but if governments and businesspeople want to, it's easy.

Big cities are designed to work day and night. There's no justification for restaurants, cinemas, theaters, concert halls and drugstores closing their doors at midnight. The investments are huge. Malls should therefore keep their stores, food courts and cinemas open until dawn. With security, of course. There would be more business profits, more jobs and more money circulating in commerce. And governments would earn more taxes.

The idea is so simple, it's hard to believe it will work. Why not give it a try?

 Everyone who was employed when the law was passed would have their monthly wages transformed into hourly wages, divided by the 144 hours they would actually work, i.e. 36 X 4 weeks, which would be one month.

 This would happen through a Social Pact between the government, companies and workers. Each would give up a little of their stake in the process. The government would reduce payroll taxes by 20%, companies would double the number of their employees, and those in employment would accept a 10% reduction in their salaries, in exchange for a reduction in hours worked, from the current 44 to 36 hours a week.

Would you like some examples of what could happen with this change, to everyone's benefit?

 WORKER: everyone would only have one six-hour shift, Monday to Saturday.
Advantages: with a rushed timetable, each worker would only spend two public transport tickets and wouldn't need to eat lunch in restaurants, they would have free time for other paid activities, to study, solve personal problems, go to banks, public bodies and have more time for shopping.

 COMPANIES: all companies, banks, industries, businesses and civil servants would extend their opening hours to twelve hours, in two six-hour shifts, starting at 7 a.m. and ending at 7 p.m., from Monday to Saturday.

Advantages: the companies' workforce would double, but in return the government would give them all a compensatory tax cut. There would be an increase in the production of goods and services.

GOVERNMENT: with a simple political decision, without any major financial investment, the government could alleviate the most serious problem a country can have, which is unemployment, and the main cause of social violence.

Advantages: increase in the number of vacancies in companies. Decrease in social pressure. Economic recovery. Increased tax collection. Improved public satisfaction.

BRAZIL: With the implementation of two work shifts, workers would have easier access to shopping during business hours. There would certainly be a considerable increase in sales and company turnover, and consequently greater development of the Brazilian economy.

The reform must be carried out so that those who take advantage of the social security system don't take advantage of it any more, don't retire at under 50, don't become vagabonds in a country of poor and miserable people.
(Fernando Henrique Cardoso, former president of Brazil)

SOCIAL SECURITY

Bum pensioners:

The new minimum wage is coming every year. It used to be May, then April, now February. The government always changes the date to suit its electoral interests. And it comes with an increase above inflation. That's good, say the optimists: it improves the lives of the poorest. Yes, but it sacrifices the lives of many others. Pensioners who receive more than the minimum wage are examples. Poor old people, they contribute all their lives to the salaries they earn, and after they retire their benefits are not adjusted at the same rate. The years go by, the amounts go down, and before long everyone will be receiving a minimum wage pension. Nothing more.

Liberal democracy, an injustice that cannot be corrected.

The government says that there is no money in the federal coffers and that giving a raise to pensioners who earn more than the minimum wage will break Social Security once and for all. Baloney. The excuse and incompetence of those who don't know how to manage the public good. There are plenty of resources, but they are diverted and stolen all the time. All you have to do is follow the reports in the press.

The government makes an average with workers, increases the minimum wage at higher rates and gives ever lower increases to inactive and retired workers who receive more than one monthly salary.

The truth is that there are many people who, up until 1992, worked for 30 or 35 years, collecting 10 or more salaries a month, retired with 7 or 8 minimum salaries, and now receive less than two minimum salaries.

There is no escaping this evil. Mathematically, it has been proven that if this adjustment policy continues, in five years' time, all pensioners who have been retired for more than 20 years will only receive a minimum wage. And those who want more income will have to pay into private pensions. This will be the consolidation of social justice by leveling pensions at the lowest benefit.

To hell with acquired rights.

Pensioners are bums, said Fernando Henrique, President of the Republic years ago. They don't work, they don't produce anything, they're old, useless, disabled people who only cause expenses for the country. For the government, it would be better if there were no pensioners, spending would be lower, the social security system would have a balance and there would be money left over to cover other deficits.

And what can be done to change this policy?

Nothing! Or almost nothing...

Can we react?

- React how? asks an elderly man. - Marches, strikes, stoppages?
It's no use, the relatives will say.
There has to be a way:
  - So let's stop working!
It doesn't work, we don't work anymore.
  - So let's go on hunger strike and go without pay for three months!
Good, the government will love it, they won't have to pay our benefits.

Unfortunately, the category is huge, there are millions of them, but they no longer produce anything for the nation. Only for their grandchildren. Pensioners and old people only cause expenses for the government, they no longer threaten the economy or public security.

This is the sad reality of life after 60 for most pensioners.

But if death hasn't come yet, there's always an innovative possibility to change things. Even at this age.

Just stop in time!

How?

That's right! Stop in time and space. Literally. And retirees have plenty of time. Time that most workers don't have. All they have to do is make good use of this available time and use the space well, by protesting, taking to the streets in groups, sitting on benches in public offices, lying on the floor of public offices, health centers, hospitals, playing truant and obstructing people passing by on bus reroutes.

Let's remember that it was after many humiliations, accusations and media reports that the BH City Council created the Master Card, which allows the elderly to leave the crowded front of the buses, pass through the turnstile and sit like the rest of the citizens in the seats at the back of the buses.

On interstate buses, the situation of disregard for the elderly has not improved. The law says that on each bus there must be two seats reserved for the elderly to travel for free and on the other seats 50% discounts on tickets. However, the companies shamelessly fail to comply and the elderly are never able to make use of these benefits.

Theaters and concert halls have already restricted half-price tickets for students and the elderly. Now, the National Congress is trying to pass a bill that would allocate only 40% of the seats in cinemas, theaters and concerts to students and the elderly.

The elderly are being outraged...

The Brazilian people are like that: they complain about everything, grumble, but prefer to sit quietly at home on the sofa watching television rather than accept an invitation to a community meeting or accompany a group of residents on a trip to a public body to ask for improvements in their neighborhood. And the elderly have time for that.

As the ancients say: there's a way out of everything in life, except death.

The way pensions are falling, if the elderly really want to attract attention, show their strength and raise public awareness, they're going to have to be quite bold and radical, take to the streets, take off their clothes and lie naked on the sidewalk of Praça Sete. During the day, hot sun. A crazy attitude, an unusual protest. It's sure to get everyone's attention, intense press coverage and who knows, some of the leaner old ladies might even get offers to take part in Big Brother or pose naked for senior citizens' magazines.

The advantage is that, unlike young people, the police aren't going to beat up a bunch of old people, shoot rubber bullets and throw tear gas bombs. Which is already a gain, if not financially, at least morally.

The suggestion is a joke, but it may be the only alternative.

Could it be that, by acting in this surreal way, the authorities will remember that pensioners and the elderly exist, adjust their benefits, provide free medicines and create preferential treatment at health centers?

When those who command lose their shame, those who obey lose their respect.
(Georg C. Lichtenberg, German satirical writer).

POLITICS AND POLITICIANS

What is politics?

Politics has several definitions: According to the Aurélio dictionary, "n. Science of the government of peoples. / Direction of a state and determination of the forms of its organization. / Set of state affairs." In the scholarly conceptualization, politics "consists of the means suitable for obtaining any advantage", according to Hobbes, or "the set of means that allow the desired effects to be achieved", for Russell, or "the art of gaining, maintaining and exercising power, government", which is the notion given by Nicolaus Machiavelli, in The Prince.

Politics is about looking after the interests of the city (polis in Greek). Every time we dedicate ourselves to doing something for the community, we are doing politics. According to Aristotle, just as it is impossible to conceive of the hand without the body, it is impossible to conceive of the individual without the state. Man is a social and political animal by nature. And if man is a political animal, it means that he has a natural need to live together in society, to promote the common good.

For the Brazilian people, however, politics is seen as politicagem, a noun that becomes an adjective, a dirty way for politicians to use the state and third parties for their own interests. Their attitudes are seen as a lack of character, soliciting voters, buying votes, unfulfilled promises, embezzling public resources, undue enrichment and administrative impropriety.

Unfortunately, Brazilians are quite right to think this about politics, which has been distorted by bad politicians. And they are the majority. Senate, Federal Chamber, Legislative Assemblies and City Councils. Each with high salaries, unacceptable perks and substandard service.

It's very common for us to complain about things, to never be satisfied with anything, to criticize the government, especially politicians. Most of the time our complaints are well-founded, we're full of reason.

Who isn't outraged, revolted or at least verbally cursing at politicians because of the constant scandals that appear in the press, showing and denouncing the thievery of various members of parliament? Not a day goes by without a new accusation, a scam, a misappropriation of funds, led by a member of parliament, a senator or a councillor.

We have to change this situation! That's what you hear everywhere.

Those who work in politics work for the people, they must think of the community, represent the interests of the community, never think of themselves.

It should be like this. But it isn't!

National Congress:

Surveys carried out by the NGO Transparência Brasil show that the Brazilian Congress is the heaviest on the public purse when compared to the budgets of 11 countries, including our neighbors Argentina and Chile, which spend much less on their parliamentarians.

Based on the amount of R$6,068,072,181.00 allocated to Congress in 2007, that's right, six billion, sixty-eight million, seventy-two thousand, one hundred and eighty-one reais, to pay for federal deputies and senators, it was concluded that Congress spends R$11,545.04 per minute to maintain this human machine that represents us.

If we compare the same spending of Argentina, Canada, Chile, France, Germany, Great Britain, Italy, Mexico, Portugal and Spain, only the United States has a bigger budget than us. The others spend much less.

With this survey, we also learned that each of the 513 federal deputies in Brasilia costs the nation's coffers R$6.6 million a year. And the 81 senators cost no less than five times as much as their colleagues, or R$33.1 million a year. All this to "work" from Tuesday to Thursday, because at weekends they have to return to their bases, to their homes, to visit their wives and children, since no one is ironclad.

Too bad for us.

According to data from 2007, imagine now, each federal deputy cost R$101,000 a month, represented by a fixed salary, various allowances, the salaries of "cabinet advisors", in reality electoral cables, which can reach 18 per deputy, and an indemnity allowance, an extra amount that the parliamentarian can use to pay for gasoline, rent for a committee in their state and other unproven expenses.

Compared to the House of Commons in Great Britain, which has a much higher per capita income than Brazil, each Brazilian MP consumes much more than the British. In the House of Representatives there, adding up salary, extras and financial aid to pay cabinet advisors, the annual cost is 168,000 pounds. Converted at R$3.78 a pound, this corresponds to just over 600,000 reais a year, which gives each British MP a monthly salary of R$50,000. Half of what a Brazilian MP earns.

And the disparity in salaries spreads across Brazil's states and municipalities, since by law, voted for by the people themselves, state deputies must earn 75% of their federal colleagues, and the same goes for councillors in relation to state deputies.

As the surveys showed, 15 Brazilian states have an annual cost per deputy higher than what a country like Italy spends, R$4 million, and where parliament is one of the most expensive in Europe. A councillor in Rio de Janeiro and São Paulo costs up to R$5 million a year.

And there are cities in Brazil, such as Rio Branco in Acre, where the annual mandate of a councillor costs R$715,000 reais. There, where the cost of a politician is the cheapest in Brazil, each of the 314,000 inhabitants contributes R$31.18, almost the same amount that French taxpayers pay to maintain their parliament. They have an income several times higher than that of the people of Acre and Brazil.

After all, what are councillors for?

Institutionally, a councillor's job is to serve the people, especially those who elected them.

To stand as a candidate, you must be Brazilian and at least 18 years old. The term of office is 4 years, with re-election, and municipal elections are held simultaneously throughout the country. The number of councillors in the municipalities ranges from 9 to a maximum of 55 for the city of São Paulo, varying according to the number of inhabitants.

Councillors do not receive salaries, but rather remuneration, which has a fixed monthly amount, plus allowances and grants. These amounts vary according to the number of inhabitants: thus, the greater the number of voters, the greater the number of councillors.

The town of Borá (SP) has the lowest number of inhabitants in the country, 807, and 09 councillors who earn salaries of 700 reais for two monthly sessions. In Belo Horizonte, there are 41 parliamentarians, who earn 15,000 reais per month and, with their allowances, each earns more than 70,000 reais per month.

Inexplicably, the city of Natal (RN) has the highest fixed salary for councillors in Brazil: 17,000 reais a month, not to mention the perks that bring the salary up to 90,000 reais. There are 29 councillors and a population of 853,000 inhabitants. São Paulo, the country's largest city, with over 11 million inhabitants, has 55 councillors, with a fixed salary of 15,000 reais.

The monthly benefits that make up the remuneration of councillors range from an office allowance to hire up to 25 assistants, an indemnity allowance, food allowance, gasoline allowance and a quota to pay cell phone bills, as well as being able to use the entire structure of the chambers for free. The only reason they don't receive a housing allowance, like state and federal deputies and senators, is because they live in their own municipality.

It would be a real shame to want this benefit again.

In order to receive all this money and perks, the councillors are obliged to "work" only 15 working days a month, attending the plenary session for three to five hours a day. All of this is backed by the Federal Constitution and by the Internal Regulations produced and approved by them.

In the city of Belo Horizonte, the third most expensive city council in the country, each of the 41 councillors cost the public coffers R$2,422,000.00 (two million four hundred and twenty-two thousand reais) in 2010, out of a municipal budget of R$100,422,000.00 (one hundred million four hundred and twenty-two thousand reais). This amount is strictly passed on every year by the City Council, taken from the taxes and fees we pay during the year.

And if there is a delay, there is a risk that the mayor will be impeached.

Can you change Brazil by voting?

No, and I'll tell you why. What's the point of choosing your candidate well, researching their past, looking at their record, thinking you've voted well, if once elected they start doing everything that other politicians have been doing for so many years? Corruption and illicit enrichment?

If we ask this question to councillors, deputies, senators, mayors, governors and the President of the Republic, they'll say yes, that we should vote, that it's a democratic act. Of course, they depend on the vote, they earn great salaries, they are in power. Let's also ask scholars, political scientists, defenders of full democracy, applied only in the First World, and surely they will all say the same thing: that it is important to vote, it is democratic, it shows that we are free, the vote is the citizen's weapon, and that only through it can we change politicians and transform social reality.

Small talk.

Propagating here in Brazil, and in South America too, that voting is good for democracy and that the vote is the citizen's weapon is pure electoral marketing and is of particular interest to the media, which plays the game of power, and to the ruling class, which walks alongside the powerful. Voting well works in First World countries, where democratic values are taught from an early age, applied and respected, people have a quality education and laws don't just remain on paper. There, anyone who governs badly, steals or embezzles goes to jail!

In Japan, corrupt politicians even commit suicide.135

Here in Brazil, when there is renewal and the elected candidate is of good character, arrives in Parliament with good projects and doesn't want to be corrupted, he is immediately looked down upon, he can't pass any projects, he goes to the lower clergy, he loses visibility. In order to stay in office and make a career of it, he ends up giving in.

Play dirty.

What's wrong in Brazil is the political system. And nobody wants to change it. It's the way candidates are elected, with proportional votes and legends, where the voter ends up putting into power a candidate they don't even know.

It's campaign financing, where donors, mostly companies, supply their favorite candidates with millions from Caixa Dois, who, once elected, are committed to returning the fortunes invested through favoritism in bids and overbilling for works.

This is a cruel political system, with an unacceptable number of senators, federal and state deputies who do not legislate on behalf of the people. Parties lack programs and party loyalty. They change parties all the time.

It's the high salaries and the perks and benefits for doing nothing that annoy the working people. And what outrages Brazilians the most is the corporatism and the special forum that the political class has, which makes them think they are better than the rest of us, voters and poor mortals.

There's no point in the media's efforts to get people to vote well and choose better. Everything will remain the same. What is needed is a movement, a chain, a national mobilization to change the Brazilian political system.

Maybe a plebiscite or a new Constituent Assembly?

It's time to stop accepting that deputies and senators earn 100,000 reais a month, and that councillors who can barely write their names receive 30, 40 or 70 thousand a month. We need to reflect and question whether we really need so many parliamentarians in the country to maintain the democratic balance.

Why spend so much on councillors in large and small towns, if the little they do, community leaders do much more and without receiving anything?

There should be as many councillors as there are neighborhoods and villages in cities. All elected by their communities. One for each neighborhood. It would be enough to give them a monthly allowance of around 3,000 reais, without any other perks, and these community leaders would certainly do everything and much more than the current councillors do.

This citizen, chosen by his or her neighborhood, would be coming and going every day to public offices seeking improvements for their localities. And much more efficiently. And the municipality would save millions paid annually to its elected councillors, who earn fortunes in direct and indirect salaries and, for the most part, do little or almost nothing for the city.

What we can't do is remain impassive, just indignant and disgusted, reading, hearing and seeing every day in the media yet another CPI that comes to nothing, yet another accusation of theft, embezzlement and corruption in the National Congress, State Assemblies and City Councils. If we don't react, more scandals will follow and we'll continue as court jesters.

Let's reform the National Congress

The honest citizen, with a clean record, who preserves his moral values, is afraid to run for any political office in Brazil. If they already had assets before being elected, or buy a house or a nice car afterwards, they'll say it was theft, embezzlement.

In Brazil, politician has become a profession, synonymous with thief, and politics politicagem, the art of cleverness, of plundering.

The difference in salary between a teacher, a doctor and a parliamentarian, be they a councillor, a member of parliament or a senator, is absurd.

There was no need for such a disparity in salaries and benefits, such inequality between what an ordinary worker earns and a citizen who is elected as a politician with the mission of defending the rights and interests of his constituents.

In the popular imagination, and the scandals help to form this awareness, every politician is dishonest, thinks only of himself and wants to get rich as quickly as possible.

Statistics compiled in 2007 by the Transparência Brasil website show that no less than 165 federal deputies, 32% of the total 513 members of the house, are facing legal proceedings. Another 30 senators, representing 37% of the 81 members of the Senate, are also accused of various crimes.

These parliamentarians are accused of crimes ranging from serious traffic offenses, embezzlement, administrative impropriety, to robbery, murder and gang formation. Many cases have already gone through the courts of appeal, confirming the accusations, some have been convicted, and yet several remain in office, with no prospect of imprisonment or removal from office.

A law popularly known as the Ficha Limpa (Clean Record) Law was voted through Congress with great difficulty, after millions of signatures were collected in a petition and on the internet. It stipulates that no candidate for any elective office can be sworn in, or even run for election, if they have been convicted in a Second Instance judgment.

Contradictorily, what we have seen are judges and courts turning a blind eye and allowing candidates with Ficha Suja to participate in elections and even take office.

The lack of punitive measures for these acts is increasing the Brazilian people's disbelief in the powers that be in the Republic. Surveys show that none of the three branches of government - the Judiciary, the Legislative and the Executive - are worthy of the respect and admiration of Brazilians. And this is terrible for building and strengthening a nation.

How can we expect a teacher or parent to send positive messages to their pupil or child that politics is serious and necessary for the country, that justice is blind and impartial, that the judges of the highest court, the STF, deserve our respect, if the examples they give us are the worst possible?

It's an arduous task.

Passing on ethical values and examples of good behavior to the younger generation is a difficult mission, given that the media are constantly reporting on scandals involving theft and the embezzlement of millions, without anyone going to prison. For young people, who are just entering the job market, there is a feeling of impunity and the message that the honest have no place and that only the clever, the rogue, the white-collar thief take advantage of everything.

The old and ever-present Gérson's Law.

Why waste time, discussions, investigations, believing that the Senate can be fixed, that we can change it in the next elections by choosing our candidates better? It's no use. The biggest problem lies in the Brazilian political system. If there is no profound political reform, no matter how honest and good-intentioned a citizen may be, if elected as a member of parliament, councillor, deputy or senator, they will soon become corrupt.

There is a gang set up in the legislative houses, a mafia that has been in place for years, which forces the parliamentarian who gets in to play the game, to vote the way "they" want, to distribute the funds, to divide up the revenue. It means accepting or being excluded from debates, not having visibility, not having a voice and presence in the media.

It's becoming a zombie.

It's past time for voters, for the Brazilian people, to demand immediate changes to the current political system, which is corrupt, to the tax system, which is unfair, and to the judicial system, which fails to punish and protects criminals.

We can no longer live with this bunch of opportunists, placed by us in Congress, state assemblies and city councils. Nobody legislates, defends or executes in the interests of the people, only their own. To say that this is what democracy is all about, that if we're not satisfied we just have to vote well, change the parliamentarian, and everything is resolved, is pure baloney.

It's the talk of those who are in power, don't want to leave, and take personal advantage of it to enrich themselves.

There's no point in simply replacing parliamentarians, because even if they were all replaced, corruption and embezzlement would continue. The problem lies in the system, in the political process, in corporatism, in the exchange of favors between the Three Powers and the Economic Power, in the way they are elected, in the campaigns, in the donations, in the perks and in the amounts that circulate without any shame between businessmen and politicians.

How can we explain the millions of reais spent on an election campaign by a single candidate, if he honestly won't receive even half of that in salaries during his four years in office? This crazy investment can only be justified with the certainty that in addition to the salaries, many commissions will appear from the billions earmarked for tendered works and the funds directed to states and municipalities.

Proposals for political reform have been discussed in Congress for years. None of them are moving forward. Only patches. There is no consensus and no interest in changing what is working. For the politicians. Because, for the population, it's past time to create a fairer and more transparent electoral system in Brazil.

Would our political institutions cease to function if, instead of 531 federal deputies and 81 senators, there were only 27 in the Senate and 27 in the Federal Chamber, two for each state? And what about the state deputies? In fact, what are they for in the states? They could be discarded.

We can no longer accept a political game where elected representatives change parties like they change shirts. Parties that have no program of action, no ideology, do not demand party loyalty from their members.

In order to be a citizen, an individual needs to have all the basic rights that the Universal Declaration of Human Rights gives them and that are always backed up by their country's constitution. And we don't have these rights.

What more can we do to transform Brazil's reality?
Wouldn't not voting, not going to the polls, paying a fine of three reais and causing a massive abstention be the most sensible response to the Brazilian authorities?

What kind of democracy is this in Brazil?

What kind of democracy is this that forces us to accept politicians like those in Congress? Could it be that, in order not to fall into an authoritarian regime, we have to swallow all kinds of theft being practiced by the majority of parliamentarians chosen by the people?

What power does the vote have in this Brazilian democracy, this obligatory tool that is said to be the voter's weapon? It only serves to elect a bunch of irresponsible and incompetent people, and has no power whatsoever to prevent abusive increases in the salaries of parliamentarians.

There seems to be no doubt that democracy is the best political regime. Winston Churchill said as much. But the time has come to rethink it as a participatory practice. We need to discuss the need for so many parliamentarians who claim to be representatives of the people.

Has anyone ever stopped to question the need and importance of so many politicians occupying seats in the National Congress?

What about the perks of Brazilian parliamentarians - does anyone in their right mind agree with the high salaries and status of life enjoyed by senators, deputies and councillors?

Is the astronomical difference between the salaries of a politician holding elected office and the monthly salary of an elementary school teacher or a public health doctor acceptable?

You can't disagree with all this and not mobilize in protests and demonstrations for change.

It's worrying!

It's worrying! When judges of the highest court argue with each other, clash and exchange insults like teenagers at the school gate. A ridiculous Supreme Court. It happened this week in Brazil.

It's worrying! When parliamentarians elected by the people, not satisfied with their high salaries, castles and lavish perks, hand out plane tickets to relatives, friends and lovers. Respect goes up in smoke.

It's worrying! When unprotected and unarmed people, especially women, pregnant women or people with children in their arms, are attacked and killed without mercy. Bandits own the streets. More than once, in many Brazilian cities.

It's worrying and even revolting! When the press discovers and publicizes that students who own luxury cars receive Prouni scholarships that were originally supposed to be for the needy. A portrait of education in Brazil.

It's worrying and disheartening! When a driver drinks, hits and kills, he denies the act, pays a small bail and is released. He doesn't even lose his license. Dry law is a lie.

It's worrying and discouraging! When bigwigs are indicted, there's plenty of evidence, recordings, videos and documents and no one goes to jail. Good lawyers and court injunctions are enough. Impunity wins. Demoralization for those who arrest, discredit for our justice system.

It's worrying, but it's what we have left! To put a stop to this state of affairs, to be indignant, not just to change parliamentarians by vote, but to demand changes in the system.

Have courage and, if necessary, go on strike, demonstrate, even stop voting. Maybe a huge abstention in the elections will have repercussions abroad, scare the politicians into taking the people seriously?

So there's no more way?

There is, but Mobilization is needed.

If there isn't a major mobilization in the country, which forces parliamentarians to listen to the protests, the virtual and street demonstrations and vote on bills that modernize the Penal Code, the Judiciary, Education, Health, the Tax System and especially a profound political reform, it will be difficult for the Brazilian economy to experience accelerated growth, with a greater supply of jobs, housing, security and social equality.

The cauldron of dissatisfaction is boiling and could explode.

And it won't be the adults, the older people who will rebel. They, us, and I include myself, are more concerned with maintaining our status, our comfort, our security in public or private employment, our pension, however derisory.

The people who are really going to be outraged, lose patience, rebel, protest, have the courage to take to the streets, with or without masks, march, demonstrate and bring about real and lasting changes in politics and society will be young people.

You can expect it. This same generation Y that uses technology like no one else, that interacts on social networks by posting "nonsense", taking "selfies", that seems alienated from social problems, will be the ones to awaken and transform the people/nation relationship in Brazil and around the world.

This revolt, however, will only come after other small but violent demonstrations by favela residents, outraged by the death of some resident, or the murder of a drug trafficker who maintains the community, culminating in the systematic burning of buses and destruction of public property.

Protests and rebellions are also expected to take place in prisons across the country, which are overcrowded and abandoned by the government. From inside the cells, criminals are already authorizing cronies and family members on the outside to rob, blow up ATMs, kidnap and kill police officers as a form of revenge.

Chaos will ensue.

Next, and we are already seeing this, the other formally organized classes of workers and businesspeople from all branches will go on strike locally and then in general, to demand from the competent authorities the changes needed to re-establish social and political order in the country.

In June 2013, we had a brief demonstration of this young Brazilian force. The youth of the internet, the hitherto alienated, decided to take to the streets and protest, they held marches and gigantic demonstrations. They came from no one knows where, no one commanded them, there were no parties in the middle, millions took to the streets to ask for change.

An unforgettable show.

In those memorable days, the demonstrators messed with the heads of politicians, authorities and scholars, who were left watching, understanding nothing, scared to death of a bloody popular uprising. They resorted to the usual strategies, called in the media, promised reforms and changes, and once again the people believed them, the demonstrations calmed down, but to this day nothing has been achieved.

Let the same demonstrations of June 2013 return.

Mobilization is needed!

And how?

It's easy, you just have to take a few initiatives, including personal transformations.

For everything you want to change in life, you need desire, need, will, motivation and action.

Firstly, wanting to change the reality of things. That's the basics.

Start by changing your reality as a person, read more, listen more, create personal goals such as getting a new job, maybe your first job, getting out of rent, buying your own home, taking care of your health, investing in your education and that of your children, if you're married.

Then, and most importantly, it's about thinking and acting collectively. To want good and progress not just for yourself and your family, but for the whole community, all your compatriots, all Brazilians. And get involved in a movement, an NGO, a community association.

No political party!

Don't be cowards. Take to the streets!
(Pope Francis to young Brazilians)

MOBILIZATION

Mobilization: the magic word:

Mobilization is a magic word because in a simple movement, in a quick articulation, it can transform everything. Making thoughts, dreams and utopias become reality, concrete, possible and applicable things, with a simple attitude of mobilization.

Mobilization: why use this word? If I'm going to talk about the desire, the need, the driving force, conscious or unconscious, that moves people to do some work, achieve goals or reach a dream, wouldn't it be better to use the term Motivation, which most speakers name their presentations after?

In fact, Motivation and Mobilization say almost the same thing. Mobilization sounds stronger, it expresses a sense of demand, of movement, it seems to provoke us to get out of immobility, out of accommodation, as if it were pushing us forward. Motivation is softer, gentler, it doesn't demand anything of us. Although both words are feminine nouns and represent the result of an attitude, for our brains, the word Mobilization refers to action, an act of moving.

That's why I chose to use the word Mobilization throughout the text.

And there's more. The word Mobilization has different applications and connotations. Used politically, it can be provocative, inducing movements, marches, strikes, demands of all kinds. In ideological discourses, it suggests transformations, changes, campaigns and strikes fear into governments. And if it doesn't change reality, at least it shakes up the complacent, forces reflection and plants seeds of transformation in people.

Mobilization is a strong and provocative term that is rarely used even in the written language of those who claim to be the people's spokespeople and change-makers: magazines and daily newspapers. It is an expression that is almost censored in radio and television news. Mobilization is a word that, due to alienation or complacency, hardly appears in the academic articles of our masters and doctors.

Even professionals who work with people's minds, who seek to transform their lives, to give their dreams a new lease of life, make little use of the word Mobilization. They prefer Motivation.

The word Mobilization shakes us up, encourages us, brings back good memories, forces us to reflect, to think that we shouldn't stand still, without moving, without participating, without fighting, without reacting.

Mobilization tells us that we need to act, for ourselves and for others, whether they are our relatives, neighbors, countrymen or citizens of the world. It's a word that provokes us to get out of our comfort zone, take to the streets, transform reality and not accept things as they are.

Mobilization through History:

With Mobilization, how many things can change in our lives, how many governments have fallen and will fall, how many others have risen to power. How humanity has progressed! If we go back in history, to the dawn of civilization, we'll discover that there was already mobilization in the Cave Men. When they were hungry, they went out to hunt for food. When they felt threatened by ferocious animals and fear of the supernatural, they mobilized and banded together to defeat the enemy.

Even at the creation of the world, Adam and Eve received Paradise from God on a platter. They got tired, protested, disobeyed and mobilized each other to adopt new behaviors that displeased the Master, culminating in their expulsion from the place that was considered the best in the world.

That leaves us.

The construction of Noah's Ark and the choice of animals to be saved from the flood was also an act of Mobilization to collect thousands of specimens of animals that would populate the new world.

The Bible offers us various accounts of Mobilization, such as that of peoples in search of better places, of the Holy and Promised Land. The story of Moses, who received from God the Tablets of the Law and the task of leading the Jewish people to the land flowing with milk and honey. So it was with Sodom and Gomorrah, who, before being destroyed for their sins and orgies, through Abraham's intercession, received two angels from God to choose from among their inhabitants at least ten people considered righteous to be saved.

It was a Mobilization.

There have been many movements and mobilizations throughout world history. Most have turned into social and political revolutions. The French Revolution in 1789 was an example of popular mobilization. It was a seizure of power by the bourgeois class, inspired by the revolutionary movements that began in the United States in 1776, passed through England, Holland, Italy, Germany and Switzerland and arrived in France. After that, the Western world was not the same. Revolutionary movements proliferated and the mobilization of the masses became constant.

Jesus Christ was a leader who mobilized people and attracted followers through his actions and speeches for a better world. He was so competent in his Mobilization that he provoked the anger and fear of the emperors, causing them to decree his death. He was a revolutionary and a winner. After 2,000 years, his teachings are still relevant today, guiding the majority of peoples on all continents.

In 1939, Adolf Hitler convinced and mobilized the German people that it would be possible to create a new order in Europe, based on Nazi principles, which defended German superiority, with the consequent extermination of races considered inferior. With this, he attacked Russia and tried to conquer Europe, starting the Second World War, which killed millions of people and only ended in 1945 with the defeat of Nazi Germany. By another mobilization of allied countries, led by the United States.

So were other more recent movements born out of the Mobilization. Like the Diretas-Já (Direct Elections) of 1989 in Brazil, in which various segments of society took to the streets demanding free elections for the president of the Republic. A similar movement was repeated in 1992, when the caras-pintadas took to the streets to demand the removal of President-elect Fernando Collor. They succeeded in impeaching him and he was removed from office.

In support of the military coup of 64 in Brazil, various sectors of society mobilized, including a number of large-circulation newspapers, religious bodies, trade unions and employers' and workers' associations. The alleged fear was that communism would take hold in the country. With the support of the media, large marches took place, such as that of the Catholic Women, which brought around 100,000 people to the streets, rosary in hand. The elected president, João Goulart, was deposed, fled the country and militarism took hold in Brazil for 21 years.

While the Military Dictatorship continued with the arrests, torture and deaths of opponents, the Mobilization stubbornly continued among the intellectual class and some politicians and labor leaders. Under pressure from so many revolts, the military issued AI-5 in December 1968 and tightened the regime even further. More arrests, torture, deaths, disappearances, the revocation of mandates and people expelled and exiled to other countries.

Mobilization continued until 1979, when political amnesty was granted and many exiles were able to return to Brazil. The military dictatorship no longer had the strength to control local and international resistance and finally, in 1985, Tancredo Neves, the first post-military regime president, was elected. He was elected but not sworn in, as he died on April 21 of the same year. In his place took office the vice-president, José Sarney, who governed until 1990.

In the popular view, Brazil is seen as a country where the people are averse to fighting, wars, rebellions and revolutions, and that everything here happens and is transformed into cabinet agreements, political arrangements, without listening to the will of the people. With the exception of a few rare moments in Brazilian history, we have to agree that we really are an excessively quiet people, with little inclination to take part in community movements, marches and public demands for our rights.

We're great at complaining, mocking and criticizing people's behavior, whether they're our relatives, neighbors, opponents of our club or members of the political class. It's just lip service. What we really like to do is chat, hang out in bars, drink beer and eat tira gosto.

Most people love to stay at home, listening to the radio, watching television, criticizing and censoring demonstrators, calling them rioters, especially if the march takes place in the street where they live. What we really like is leaning out of the window, passively and without interaction, watching those brave little cats on the streets, with their painted faces, some masked, most of them young, protesting, getting beaten up, demanding rights on behalf of everyone.

Unfortunately, that's how we are, it's cultural, we only mobilize for something when the mainstream press is in front of us and calls us out. Then we go happily and innocently, like children after sweets and toys. Obedient, without contesting anything. And we do what they decide is good for the country... It was like that when Jango fell, when the military dictatorship was established in 1964, when Fernando Collor was elected in 1990 and when he was impeached two years later with the media movement Caras Pintadas.

Because of the lack of authentic leaders in our society.

It's a pity that since then, dozens of years later, no other real mobilization has taken place in the country. Other presidents have been elected, thousands of politicians have been sworn into office, several scandals have been repeated, billions of reais have been embezzled, impunity, corruption and violence unchecked. And we did nothing to show our indignation.

We remain passive, just complaining and not acting.

In all that time, we only campaigned for the vote and implementation of the Ficha Limpa project, which proposed preventing people who had committed any crime from running for and holding any public office. More than a million signatures were collected in person and another three million obtained online.

The bill was approved, became law, entered into force, we won the battle, but we didn't win the fight.

Disgruntled, those affected by Ficha Limpa have appealed to the Supreme Court, won deadlines, delayed proceedings and had their sentences postponed indefinitely.

Some convicts died without serving their sentences. Many candidates are still elected and in power.

Powerful people who don't respect the people and defy the law.

We lack a culture of mobilization:

Against the mobilization, there is the disbelief, the disillusionment of most people in any attempt to change the state of things, the reality we live in. We prefer to whine, get by with things, ask for help from here and there, get an overdraft, screw over others, not pay debts, get on the SPC, evade taxes.

Almost nobody wants to mobilize to improve their lives. It's a waste of time, it won't lead to anything, is what you hear in attempts to bring groups together and propose effective actions.

Anyone who works with communities, groups of people, whether they are from outlying neighborhoods, school environments, religious or political movements, knows how difficult it is to sensitize participants to become actively involved in actions for personal demands and civil rights. People want solutions to their problems and needs, but are unwilling to give up part of their time to seek results.

Complaints, demands and lack of interest are the most common attitudes at most condominium meetings, whether residential or commercial. There's no way to get shopkeepers out of their stores and residents out of their apartments once a month to discuss improvements and cost control in the buildings where they work or live. Few go, and the meetings almost always end in fights.

It's more difficult to convince residents of neighborhoods to attend meetings of community associations, which fight to achieve urban improvements with public bodies. At election time, some dreamers even attend, believing the candidates' promises.

Disillusioned, they never go to meetings again.

Despite the efforts of some idealists, NGOs close their doors due to a lack of volunteers, churches find it difficult to form social action groups and Local Health Commissions can't get people to form slates for board elections. Then come the complaints about continuity, criticism of people who remain at the head of organizations and social movements for years.

There is no renewal, for lack of selfless, interested people.

The lack of interest and commitment on the part of the community is worrying and leads us to the conclusion that Brazil's historical process is the cause of so much alienation from social movements and the search for citizens' rights. It's an affliction that seems to affect all of Latin America, as we rarely see any of these countries promoting deeper and more organized mobilizations aimed at seeking better living conditions for their people.

Everyone knows, or at least should know, since the written, spoken and televised press and the internet report daily on the chaotic state in which the Brazilian nation lives. Although the country has developed a lot in the last two decades, the social gap is still wide, and we are almost half a century away from the level of equality of countries in Europe and the United States.

Around here we have the feeling that wrong is right and right is wrong. So said former player and commentator Kafunga. There are difficulties and bureaucratic hurdles to any undertaking or attempt to innovate. And to get around the difficulties, there's always the Brazilian way. It's a friendship here, a referral there, a bribe in the hand of a civil servant or policeman and the fine is not collected and the infraction annulled. There are many laws in the country and most of them are poorly enforced.

Or rather, it's almost always applied to the underprivileged.

The press in the lead:

We like mobilizations when they are led by a major media outlet. Then, if called upon, we even take to the streets, protest, shout and get beaten up for any cause. Even if we don't know what that cause is or who really cares.

Authentic Mobilization has the magical power to transform everything that you don't want to remain as it is. Whether on a personal, governmental, political or social level. Mobilization can bring down walls, dictators, the corrupt and unjust economic policies. You just have to want to. No one can hold back the will of the people when they know what they want. Neither by speech nor by violence.

The Arab Spring:

In recent years, we've seen the fall of dictatorial governments around the world, which had imagined themselves to be firm and dominant, secure in power for decades. People who had never known revolts or imagined themselves to be organized are suddenly taking to the streets, demonstrating, demanding political and economic change and showing that they want freedom. Of thought and action.

It all started with the fall of the regimes in Tunisia and Egypt, followed by the overthrow and death of Muahamar Gaddafi in Libya and more recently the popular uprising against the Syrian government. It took on the name of the Arab Spring and has sparked popular uprisings all over the world.

Tunisian dictator Zine Al-Abidine Ben Ali resigned from power on January 14, 2011, after almost a month of violent street protests, through a movement called for by bloggers and users of Twitter and the social network Facebook. Through cell phones, images reached international TV stations showing the world the riots and deaths that were taking place on the streets of the capital Tunis.

Constant riots are taking place in Athens, Egypt, Madrid in Spain, Kiev in Ukraine, and looting and street vandalism in cities that are examples of civility, such as Paris and London. No one is immune to protests and demonstrations anymore. In India, China and Russia, even with restrictions on the press, there are constant reports of people clashing with the government.

Press censorship has always been one of the most important weapons of dictatorial regimes. In many countries in the Arab world, where authoritarian governments control newspapers and radio and TV stations, internet activism has become the only way for citizens to express their frustrations and indignation.

The wealth and corruption of the ruling elite, combined with religious disputes, have been instrumental in fueling revolts in countries like Tunisia and Egypt. Constant acts of corruption, official misconduct and disrespect for human rights have been the basis of popular protests in India and China. The lack of opportunities and jobs for young people and the falling standards of living of the middle class have been common themes in public demonstrations in Spain, Greece, Israel, Chile and Venezuela.

Interestingly, many of the countries hit by the turmoil of the demonstrations had their populations passively accept growing social inequality as a price worth paying in exchange for rapid economic growth. Even without income distribution.

Globalization has substantially raised the incomes of the rich, while at the same time creating an international labour market that pushes down the wages of less qualified workers, especially in Western countries. China is largely responsible for this.

And this same globalization that has interacted economies has fostered the emergence of uncontrolled internet communication networks, which allow ideas, texts and images of protests, demonstrations and revolts to travel the world in seconds.

We are living through a new revolutionary period in the world. Instead of the urban guerrillas, attacks and armed struggles in search of ideological transformations that plagued the world until the 1970s, today hackers are breaking into computers, distributing viruses, people are protesting, demonstrating, rebelling, taking to the streets, demanding political and economic changes that will bring immediate improvements to their essential needs for food, education, health, work, housing and security, as promised by universal human rights laws.

Brazil is fashionable, one of the best places to invest, say the experts, just like China and India, other emerging economies in the world. Here, however, there is still a lot of bureaucracy, too many taxes, inequality and endemic corruption. In all spheres of society. The country is growing less than it should, and wealth is not distributed as it should be.

Every day, economic power becomes more concentrated in the hands of the rich and powerful.

Social Transformations:

We are living through a new era in world society. The big players in the economy are falling, the small ones are rising. Brazil goes with them. We haven't grown as expected, high taxes, excessive bureaucracy and poor infrastructure are all obstacles.

We have come a long way in terms of social policies, human rights, labor rights and civil rights. On paper, our laws are examples to the world.

The Statute for the Protection of Children and Adolescents (ECA) and the Statute for the Protection of the Elderly (Estatuto de Proteção ao Idoso) are considered by experts to be the most advanced laws in the world when it comes to providing basic rights and special assistance to children, young people and people over the age of 60.

How nice it is to be a teenager and not be punished for crimes, or to be old enough not to pay for buses and have half-price tickets to theaters and music shows.

Although they don't always work well in practice, we have specific laws, which many First World countries don't have, that protect consumers, that strictly punish racist expressions, that protect women from threats and aggression from their husbands and partners. The Maria da Penha Law is one of them. Others, such as those banning nicknames, bullying and condemning acts of homophobia, are in Congress to be approved.

Gay parades, free abortion, demonstrations in favor of homosexual freedom, same-sex marriage and the adoption of children by male or female couples are a reality, part of our daily lives.

166

Lesbians and gays are starring in soap operas, campaigns against homophobia are taking to the streets, minorities are marching to demand recognition and rights.

It's impossible to be against it.

We can be the first in the world:

Despite everything, Brazil is still the best place in the world to live. Anyone who goes abroad can see that. All you have to do is look critically. Even with all the political shenanigans here, with all the excessive taxes on companies and individuals, with all the violence on the streets, in traffic, in homes, against citizens.

When we travel abroad, whether for business or pleasure, we are amazed at how organized things are, charmed by the discipline of the people, the politeness of the traffic, the cleanliness of the streets, the almost perfect functioning of public services, the respect for and compliance with the law.

And we talked:

- It could be like this in Brazil!

And it could! We have everything here. Good weather, lots of space, plenty of natural resources, happy, optimistic and receptive people. Abroad, although wealthy, people are grumpy, not very cheerful, too disciplined and don't always welcome tourists. Especially Latin Americans.

I've visited several European countries, as well as the USA, where I've lived and then gone on trips. I've seen beautiful cities and breathtaking landscapes, I've studied ancient and medieval, modern and contemporary history. I had fun as a child at Disney, sailed in the gondolas of romantic Venice, saw the ruins of Pompeii, the museums of the Roman Empire, the treasures of the Vatican, and was horrified to see the Dachau concentration camp in Germany, the site of the horrors of the Second World War.

Almost perfect cities, clean streets, transport to choose from, buses, trains, metro, streetcars. Rivers without any pollution, clean enough to make you want to drink from them. Strong security, disciplined people on the streets, little conversation, almost no noise. They seem robotized.

Tourism is an industry abroad. Here, it's all fun and high prices. In Europe, it's the main source of income. In any form of transport, bus, train, metro or ship, whatever the route, the majority of travelers are always Brazilians. They come from all states and social classes. You don't even have to ask. Just observe their manner, listen to their voice, their irreverence. And how they buy! Exciting and unimaginable.

A sign of the new times, financing at will, credit cards maxed out.
If we want to, we can be the first and the biggest in the next 20 years. No doubt about it. We just need to want it, have the political will and invest heavily in infrastructure. We need good roads, large airports, railroads, subways and fast transport of what we produce. That's what we have abroad. And we don't have it here!

How to mobilize:

Mobilizing, moving, passing or carrying news from one place to another, from person to person, was much more difficult back then. There wasn't all this paraphernalia of technological communication tools that we have today. Imagine the dawn of civilization. There was no writing and people barely knew how to speak. To understand each other, they used gestures, signs and mime. Then came cave drawings, messages in the shape of animals, the sun and the moon, mail on horseback.

Today, in the 21st century, advanced technology offers us a wide variety of communication tools. In an instant, without leaving our place, we can communicate with people in the most distant places on the planet. And even beyond, as in the interplanetary journeys made by the great nations.

Since the invention of the telegraph in 1844, the world has shrunk and distances have become shorter. Along came radio, cinema and television, which brought people even closer to what was happening in other parts of the world.

In the 1960s, man went to the moon and the world's third and greatest technological revolution took place. Since then, various inventions and electronic devices have emerged. From telex to fax, from AM to FM radio, from twin-engine to supersonic, from TV to digital, from vinyl to DVD, from landlines to cell phones. All seeking interaction. Of people and businesses.

With the Internet, everything has been revolutionized...

Suddenly we have everything in our hands, modern tools, easy shopping and access, and we've forgotten how to Mobilize. We get comfortable, we are amazed by everything. Cell phones, USB sticks, smartphones, iphones, websites, blogs, twitter, facebook, we're afraid. Of everything and everyone.

They invaded our privacy.

We've managed to shorten distances, to break down communication barriers, but we've chosen to stay away from our neighbors. We avoid physical presence, preferring virtual interaction. Better an e-mail contact, a Skype call, a tweet on your cell phone. Physical involvement, face-to-face emotions, eye-to-eye are dangerous. We avoid showing our faces.

Sometimes we expose ourselves too much on social media.

The people don't know how strong they are:

If there were capable and well-intentioned leaders, the educated people would quickly change the political and social situation in Brazil. And there could be many actions.

Just press it.

If so many people are living on the streets, without a roof over their heads, without housing, it would be enough to gather in front of the state government headquarters in Minas Gerais, in the Administrative City, and stand there, shouting protest phrases, camping out in tents, waking up and sleeping for days, weeks and even months, and surely the authorities would take action.

If there were no aggressions or threats to storm the palace, the police wouldn't beat up or arrest protesters. And, overcome by the insistence and repercussions of the protests, the authorities might become sensitized to the demands and respond to them. After all, politicians and authorities claim to be representatives of the people. So let's collect.

Through mobilization and protest, as a civilized people, we can obtain from the public authorities everything that the Constitution guarantees us and that is denied to us for various reasons. With these tools, we have the right to dispatch politicians who do wrong, judges who don't decide and corrupt rulers who don't know how to manage the public good and who claim not to have the resources to meet the basic needs of the population.

The way is to mobilize!

Mobilizing isn't just about taking to the streets and protesting. It's also about offering alternatives to solve problems, collaborating, giving new ideas, even if they take time or are never used.

This is a time of crisis. Real or not, everyone is talking about it. Wouldn't it be time for governments, public entities and state-owned companies, most of which are monopolists, to immediately suspend the investments they make in paid advertising in the national media and in sponsoring soccer clubs?

It's worth asking: why and for whom do companies like Petrobras, Cemig and Copasa advertise their activities if they have no competitors? Why do we have to know that the oil, electricity and drinking water of state-owned companies are the best in the country, if only they produce and sell the products? By dispensing with advertising, they would save many millions of reais and avoid the hasty and always cruel dismissal of thousands of workers who have nothing to do when the international crisis appears and incompetent management stands out.

We have to be bold and propose changes. For example, we need to question the importance of politicians to us, propose transformations and demand that Congress make far-reaching reforms to the current political system, the judicial system and the national tax system, with a view to correcting excesses, omissions and injustices.

There is no other way for the people to get the benefits they need, and which are the duty of those in power, than through pressure, protests, peaceful and constant demonstrations.

Demonstrating is the best way:

Seeing the scandals that are being repeated in Brazil, we absolutely cannot remain inert. We need to protest, demand action and solutions from our authorities. We cannot be afraid. We should be afraid, and rightly so, of the insecurity that surrounds our commute from home to work, from our evening studies to our return home, when bandits mug us and stray bullets hit us.

We can't accept police killing people, police arresting people and the courts convicting and allowing appeals with the defendants free. Even when the crime presents incontrovertible evidence and the offender is arrested in the act. This generates disbelief in the victims and does nothing to strengthen institutions. What we see is an ever-increasing disdain and distancing of citizens from politicians and politics. Politicians and thieves now have the same value for Brazilian voters. And that's a bad thing.

Grain by grain, attitude by attitude, contact by contact, we can change the Brazilian reality. Let's hold virtual protests, on the internet, sending emails, text messages on cell phones, using twitter, blogs, social networking communities like facebook, whatsapp and others. After all, technology allows us to interact instantaneously with people like never before.

It's even better if we can protest in person, peacefully, constantly, for months on end, without violence, as well-educated people do and should do. It's healthy to take to the streets, hold marches, form groups outside banks, stores and public utilities to demand our rights.

It makes an impact and it almost always works to gather many people, dozens, hundreds, thousands, and stand outside banks and stores with banners making demands. How good it is for democracy for people to go into the galleries of town halls and legislative assemblies and put pressure on councillors and deputies to vote on projects of public interest and not to approve honorary citizen titles and street names.

This is healthy, democratic and brings support from more conservative people.

The time is ripe for change:

Sometimes I keep thinking, making conjectures in my mind, imagining what we could do, in concrete terms, to transform this chaotic Brazilian social reality for the better. Revolt by arms, never! Supporting some crazy person or group willing to carry out a coup, much less. We've already made many of these mistakes and the most recent one, the Military Regime, is 50 years old.

We are still reaping the results of this oppression today.

What to do then? Stay still? Keep quiet? Accept that things continue as they are, accumulate a few more decades of economic backwardness, continue in misery? We can't commit this atrocity with our principles, practicing a "haraquiri" with our beliefs. We need to react. But how, if there are so many corporate interests at stake, if nobody wants to change anything, if for many it's better to carry on as we are?

We need to mobilize!

That's right! We have to come together, rich people, poor people, men, women, young people, adults, students, teachers, bosses and employees, around an idea for change that is consistent, objective, that has already been successfully tried and approved, and that we know in practice will work, that can transform Brazil.

In June 2013, young people on the internet started an unprecedented movement that has left them feeling nostalgic and with lessons to learn. It's a pity that the movement couldn't be repeated in the same way, with the same number of people, and without the participation of rioters and unwanted political banners.

But the dream isn't over, the giant hasn't fallen asleep, it's just dozing off, hope continues, and who knows, maybe this year or next, we'll have new, grandiose and constant demonstrations that will force Brazilian politicians to make the changes that the people are asking for and which are not being met.

We can't go against the demonstrations:

We must fully support protests in the streets. As long as they are peaceful. And we can't accept our young people being silenced. As was the case during the dictatorship, many organizations and parts of the media are beginning to take a stance against the demonstrations, saying that the participants are just rioters, vandals, vagabonds, without disclosing that the majority are students, teachers, workers and trade unionists. This is the protesters' moment. They are doing today what many of us did during the years of lead in Brazil.

We were called communists, subversives, terrorists.

It's time to clean up the country and demand deep and immediate transformations. Enough with the deceit, impunity, corruption, insecurity, political deviance and malfeasance. We, the older generation, the fathers, mothers and grandparents of these young people who are mobilizing on social networks and in the streets, can only applaud them and warn them to avoid confrontations and attacks on police officers and not to cause damage to public and private property.

The first battle has been won. Now what?

No one is satisfied with the quality and regularity of mass transportation, be it bus, train or metro. We need to invest more in this sector.

Health care is precarious, there are so many queues for appointments at public health centers and people lying in hospital corridors waiting for an opening. It's inhuman.

Education has huge flaws, poor teaching, teachers without incentives and fair salaries.

Public security only exists on paper, bandits take over the streets and citizens have to remain caged and fearful in their homes and businesses. And so on and so forth goes the rosary of dissatisfaction with the federal, state and municipal governments. And politicians in general.

Everyone knows the root, the origin, the source of the great evils that afflict the Brazilian people: the current political system. It is in it and through it that the embezzlement of funds, corruption, the game of self-interest, make-believe, unfulfilled promises, the receipt of extremely high salaries, spurious agreements between parties and rulers to pass laws and perpetuate themselves in power take place.

So it's the Brazilian political system that should be the focus of public and peaceful demonstrations from now on. Let's take to the streets and demand an immediate and far-reaching reform from the National Congress:

-Deep political reform;

-Complete tax reform;

-Judicial Reform;

-The end of compulsory voting in elections:

-Reduce and stipulate a fixed, reasonable and transparent salary for all parliamentarians, from councillors to senators.

-Reducing the cost of the public machine by cutting 39 ministries to a maximum of 15:

-Create party loyalty laws for politicians, preventing them from switching parties at any time.

And for all of this to become a reality, a Special, Popular and Specific Constituent Assembly must be called, suspending the current mandates of all parliamentarians and opening up elections for candidates for constituent positions. And those elected would have two years in office to discuss the proposals with society, vote and enact the changes in the new Federal Constitution.

It is to be hoped that whoever is in power has the ears to hear the clamor coming from the streets, and makes the profound reforms that the country needs. If there is too much delay, let's not be alarmed if civil leaders, businesspeople, doctors, teachers and other professional bodies join forces with judges and military personnel of the highest court and rank, both active and reserve, no longer for a military coup, but to democratically force the government authorities to implement the changes demanded by society and put Brazil back on the path of progress, justice and ethical and moral values.

The time is ripe for protests and demonstrations:

Yes, it's time for protests, strikes and stoppages. Various organizations, unions and segments of society need to take to the streets and protest, demand labor rights, better working conditions in their activities, close streets, paralyze traffic and commerce.

No one can passively accept the decisions and impositions of the authorities. Subway workers have to stop trains and subways, airline workers have to stop planes from going up, doctors have to stop seeing patients, reject professionals from other countries and take their places in public health.

Will it be hard for the people? Yes! Stoppages, traffic jams, difficulties getting to work, buses, trains and subways on strike. This is the price you have to pay for change in the country.

Brazil is in social turmoil, boiling over, and this, although worrying, has a positive side, it brings hope to all of us, provokes change and shows that despite the resistance, there are people and groups mobilizing, with a clean face or in hiding, in the streets or on social networks, looking for new proposals to transform our country.

As Pope Francis said, we should congratulate the young people who take to the streets, who hold protests and demonstrations, and sometimes even go overboard. These young people today are the dreamers and revolutionaries we once were, when we brought about social change in the 1960s, fighting and overcoming prejudice, dictatorships and repression.

Don't expect many people over the age of 60 to be at these demonstrations, like me, who maintain the revolutionary spirit, but today I'm just writing and suggesting mobilizations that can bring about profound changes.

This generation Y of the 21st century, which dominates the internet and interacts and confabulates through social networks, is the one that will break paradigms, overthrow myths and prejudices, put an end to differences and privileges between people, workers and classes that are still inexplicably privileged, such as the caste of Brazilian politicians.

The Pope doesn't like it, he said so for everyone to hear, he prefers the revolutionary. In a good way, of course. Let young people remain indignant, let them not accept things as they are, let them demand change now, let them hold protests, demonstrations, always peaceful, without gratuitous violence.

The Holy Father is gone, we're left here, the politicians have done nothing, they keep promising, Brazil is waiting for change, which can't take much longer.

So how about getting back on the streets?

In life, everything has a time. A time to be born, to live and to die. This time in Brazil is one of change and transformation.
Time to use the Magical Power of Mobilization.

THE END

Of this book, not of dreams.

About Author
Flávio Henrique

"I am a visionary entrepreneur and seasoned technologist with over two decades of experience in the IT industry. My career journey has been marked by a relentless pursuit of excellence, spanning web hosting, cloud computing, cybersecurity, and web community building. As the founder of successful ventures, I have a proven track record of creating and leading technology-driven companies. Additionally, my active involvement in the iMasters community, which boasts over 450,000 web developers and professionals, reflects my commitment to fostering knowledge sharing. My expertise extends from strategic business development and leadership development and infrastructure management. With a comprehensive understanding of technology ecosystems and a passion for innovation, I am poised to drive success in dynamic business environments."